Etiquette and Culture in Western Society

本书详细介绍了西方社会的礼仪规范和相关文化背景，旨在帮助人们在对外交往中充分展现中国公民良好的礼仪素养和精神面貌。全书共分为12章，内容涵盖了西方礼仪文化概述、见面礼仪、人际交往礼仪、文书礼仪、公共场所行为礼仪、餐饮礼仪、着装礼仪、婚俗礼仪、丧葬礼仪、商务礼仪、禁忌礼仪和体态礼仪。本书在介绍西方社会礼仪规范的同时深入挖掘其后的文化根源和背景知识，每一章正文之后的情景对话和补充阅读材料都尽量保持了英语的原汁原味，有助于读者在阅读中学习地道的语言。

本书可作为高校学生的选修课教材及英语、对外汉语等专业的拓展课程教材，也可作为课外阅读书籍，同时也适合出国留学人士和广大英语爱好者学习使用。

西方社会礼仪与文化

– 东方剑桥应用英语系列 –

范 冰 著

Etiquette and Culture in Western Society

ZHEJIANG UNIVERSITY PRESS
浙江大学出版社

PREFACE 前言

我国自古就是礼仪之邦，礼仪文化可谓博大精深。随着时代的不断进步以及全球化的影响，科技、文化、教育都日益趋向现代化和国际化，礼仪文化作为社会文明的标志之一，也需要作出相应的变革。现代礼仪文化既要继承中华礼仪传统，同时也要在与西方文明的学习交融中不断推进。中国加入世贸组织之后，尤其在全球化的今天，西方礼仪文化更是成了热门话题。如今，越来越多的国人走出国门，或留学，或旅游，或进行国际交流，或从事商务活动。人们越来越深刻地意识到西方礼仪文化知识在对外交往中的重要性。正如习近平总书记在党的二十大报告中所指出的："深化文明交流互鉴，推动中华文化更好走向世界"，在古今中西的文化激荡中，我们既要传承优良的传统礼仪文化，保持中华礼仪文化的独特性，又要以开放的姿态面对与吸收西方礼仪文化元素，传承与弘扬我们的礼仪文化。这样不仅能让我们在对外交往活动中充满自信、处变不惊，展现中国公民良好的精神风貌，还能加深与世界各国人民的友谊和交流，增进彼此的信任和了解，提高我国的国际地位和威望，从而确立中华文化的感染力，使中华文明屹立于世界民族之林。

鉴于此目的，作者深感十分有必要出一本全面、实用、契合时代发展的现代西方社会礼仪文化方面的书籍。在作者多年教授"西方礼仪文化"课程的基础上，经过近两年的准备、资料搜集和撰写，倾注了作者无数心血和汗水的《西方社会礼仪与文化》终于即将面世了。为使本书的内容准确实用，在本书的撰写过程中，作者尽可能多地查阅了外文的第一手资料，并反复求证，以避免受译文的误导而引起的曲解或产生不准确的表述。

本书详细介绍了西方社会的礼仪规范和相关文化背景，旨在帮助人们了解西方社会，尤其是欧美国家的礼仪文化知识以及在对外交往中的一些国际惯例。全书一共分为12章，内容涵盖了现代西方社会礼仪与文化的方方面面，包括西方文化礼仪概述、见面礼仪、人际交往礼仪、文书礼仪、公共场所行为礼仪、餐饮礼仪、着装礼仪、婚俗礼仪、丧葬礼仪、商务礼仪、禁忌礼仪和体态礼仪。每一章都分为三个部分：第一部分为礼仪文化知识的介绍，文后列有详细的生词表及练习；第二部分为情景对话，提供一些在不同场景下的对话范例；第三部分为与本章内容相关的补充阅读材料，基本选自外报外刊。本书在介绍西方社会礼仪规范的同时深入挖掘其后的文化根源和背景知识，每一章正文之后选取的情景对话和补充阅读材料都尽量保持了英语的原汁原味，有助于读者在阅读中学习地道的语言与表达。本次重印，我们在每章的最后增加了一个二维码，内容涵盖了对应中国传统礼仪文化中的一些英文表达，以期帮助学生学会用英语传播中国文化，讲好中国故事。

从酝酿本书到完成初稿乃至定稿的过程丝毫不亚于期待和孕育一个新生命，虽然历尽艰辛，但最终充满喜悦而自豪地迎来它的降临。在这一过程中，首先要特别感谢美籍外教Michael Au，他花费了大量的时间和精力对全书的语言、内容进行了仔细的审阅修改；其次要感谢卢睿蓉博士对本书的撰写提出的许多宝贵意见；最后要感谢家人在背后默默无私的支持。没有他们的支持和帮助，也不会有本书今天的模样。

本书可作为高校学生的大学英语选修课教材及英语、对外汉语等专业的拓展课程教材，也可作为学生的课外阅读书籍，同时也适合出国留学人士和广大英语爱好者学习使用。

范　冰

2023年6月

CONTENTS 目录

Chapter 4

Chapter 5

Chapter 6

Chapter 1
Outline of Western Culture and Etiquette

西方文化礼仪概述

在本章中，你将了解到：
- 西方的概念
- 文化的构成
- 西方文化逻辑和思维方式
- 西方社会礼仪的起源

Intensive Reading

1.1 The Conception of West

The earliest division of East and West based on cultural perceptions can be traced back to a series of great wars. From 492 BC to 479 BC, during the Persian Wars between Ancient Greece and the Persian Empire, the Greeks began to realize their difference from the Persians in geography, custom, religion, politics, language and so on. Since then, they had formed the conception of East and West and began to regard themselves as Western people in order to distinguish them from the Eastern people. Greek historian Herodotus (479 BC–431 BC), reported in his *Histories*, "…with the Persians possessing Asia and its various barbarian peoples, and thinking Europe and the Greeks being distinct from them…" This is an earlier division of east and west culture. As the Father of History, Herodotus' view had a great impact on Hegel and other philosophers.

After more than 2,000 years' evolution, "the West" has become a concept with a fixed meaning in different periods. In terms of its geographical, economical and political sense, the West refers to Europe and Northern America including the United States and Canada. Being observed from the perspective of history of European culture, the West can be divided into three cultural systems, (i) the system of Mediterranean Sea, which is the origin of western culture; (ii) the system of Western Europe, which is the main part of "the Atlantic Culture;" (iii) the system of Eastern Europe. In fact, the three cultural systems had gradually integrated since the Renaissance, and consisted of a big realm of western culture. Apart from Europe, western culture also includes Northern America and Australia, which could be seen as the fourth component of western culture.

In a nutshell, the West mainly refers to the cultural pattern which originates from the Greek and Roman culture and takes modern industries as its economic modes. Besides, its people generally believe in Christianity.

1.2 What Is Culture?

When it comes to the word "culture," what will you think of? The word "culture" has many different meanings. For many people it refers to an appreciation of good literature, music, art, and food. For a biologist, it is likely to be a colony of bacteria or other microorganisms growing in a nutrient medium in a laboratory Petri dish. Defining culture is a really tough job, because scholars have diverse understandings of it. However, for anthropologists and other behavioral scientists, **culture is the full range of learned human behavior patterns**. The term was first used in this way by the English anthropologist pioneer Edward B. Tylor in his book *Primitive Culture*, which was published in 1871. Tylor said that culture is "That complex whole which includes knowledge, belief, art, law, morals, custom, and any other capabilities and habits acquired by man as a member of society." Since Tylor's time, more than 200 different definitions have come up, but this concept of culture has become the central focus of anthropology.

Culture is a powerful human tool, and meanwhile it is quite fragile. It is constantly changing and easily lost because it exists only in our minds. Our written languages, buildings, and other man-made things are merely the products of culture. They are not culture in themselves. For instance, the broken pots and other artifacts of ancient people that archaeologists uncover are only material remains. But they reflect cultural patterns—they are things that were made and used through cultural knowledge and skills. American linguist Levine (1993) has compared culture to an iceberg, most of which is hidden underwater. Culture hides more than it reveals. Language, food, and appearance are aspects clearly visible to us. However, communication styles, beliefs, attitudes, values, perceptions, etc., are interacting beyond our conscious awareness.

Generally speaking, there are three levels of culture that are parts of our learned behavior patterns and perceptions. Most obviously, it is the body of cultural traditions that distinguish our specific society. When people speak of Chinese, French or Canadian culture, they are referring to the shared language, traditions, and beliefs that set apart each of these peoples from the others. In most cases, the reason why people share our culture is that they were raised by parents and other family members who have it.

The second level of culture is a *subculture*. In complex, diverse societies in which people have come from many different parts of the world, they often retain much of their original cultural traditions. As a result, they are likely to be part of an identifiable subculture in their new society. The shared cultural traits of subcultures set them apart from the rest of their society. Examples can be easily found in ethnic groups in the United States such as Vietnamese Americans, African Americans, and Mexican Americans. But in such a society, a subculture and the dominant national culture might have influence upon each other. As days wear on, the cultural differences between their members blur and eventually disappear. The subculture ceases to exist except as a group of people who claim a common ancestry.

The third level of culture consists of *cultural universals*. These are learned behavior patterns that are shared by all of humanity collectively. No matter where people live in the world, they share these universal traits. Although all cultures have these and possibly many other universal traits, different cultures have developed their own specific ways of carrying out or expressing them. For instance, people in all cultures have their tabooed utterances toward others by calling them animal names with abusive meanings. However, these animal names are diverse in different languages.

1.3 Cultural Logic of Westerners

Cultural logic refers to the established thought pattern and cognitive style based on the logical system in a culture. It is the maincenter of cultural behaviors, which means all kinds of cultural phenomena are directly related to the logic behind culture. To some extent, the social world is an ecological complex in which individuals personally embody cultural meanings and knowledge—both linguistic and non-linguistic—via commonly accessible semiotic structures. This interpersonal ecology bridges realms which are the subject matter of both anthropology and linguistics. It allows the public maintenance of a system of assumptions and counter-assumptions among individuals as to what is mutually known, in general and in any particular context. The mutual assumption of particular cultural ideas provides human groups with common premises for predictably convergent inferential processes. This process of people collectively using effectively identical assumptions in interpreting each other's actions is termed cultural logic.

The ancient Greek logic system had an unparallel influence on western culture and thought pattern. The Greek philosopher Aristotle is the idea collector of Greek logic, which is of great significance towards the development of Western cultures. Aristotle's most famous achievement as a logician is his theory of inference, traditionally called the *syllogism*. That theory is in fact the theory of inferences of a very specific sort: Inferences with two premises (i.e., a major premise and a minor premise), each of which is a categorical sentence, having exactly one term in common, and having as conclusion a categorical sentence the terms of which are just those two terms not shared by the premises. According to Aristotle, each of the premises is in the form "All A are B" and "No A are B," which are termed universal propositions; or "Some A are B" and "Some A are not B," which are termed particular propositions. Each of the premises has one term in common with the conclusion: In a major premise, this is the *major term* (i.e., the predicate of the conclusion); in a minor premise, it is the *minor term* (the subject of the conclusion). For example:

Major premise: All men are mortal.

Minor premise: All Greeks are men.

Conclusion: All Greeks are mortal.

Each of the three distinct terms represents a category. In the above example, "mortal" is the major term; "Greeks," the minor term. The premises also have one term in common with each other, which is known as the *middle term*. In this example, "men" is the middle term. Both of the premises are universal, as is the conclusion.

Another example is as follows:

Major premise: All mortals die.

Minor premise: Some men are mortals.

Conclusion: Some men die.

Here, the major term is "die," the minor term is "men," and the middle term is "mortals." The major premise is universal; the minor premise and the conclusion are particular.

Aristotle's logic reveals as well as represents the striking feature of western thought, which is to extract identity from universal things, and evolve it into laws. This principle judged by identity has become the mainstream of western rationality.

In addition to the ancient Greek logic system, western thought pattern is also greatly influenced by another logic—divinity logic. Western culture at a given time was affected by the governing class. In its evolution, the medieval divinity logic is a special period, in which the Western cultural logic served Christian divinity and became a tool for divinity education. Although the divinity logic had been a part of history, it would not disappear as a tradition and has an inherent link with western thought in reality.

Aristotle (384 BC–322 BC)

1.4 What Is Etiquette?

The French word *étiquette* used to mean "keep off the grass." It was in the 18th century that French King Louis XIV used to invite people to his palace for parties and festivals. His gardener at Versailles was faced with a serious problem: He could not stop members of the nobility from trampling about in the delicate areas of the King's garden. He finally attempted to dissuade their unwanted behavior by posting signs in French called "etiquette" which warned them to "Keep off the grass, don't walk on the flowers." However, the dukes and duchesses walked right past these signs. When this course of action failed, the King himself had to issue an official decree that no one could go beyond the bounds of the signs. Later, the name "etiquette" was given to a ticket for court functions that included rules regarding where to stand and what to do.

Over time the word "etiquette" has evolved, which came to mean all the little signs that help us know what to do in new and different situations. And in even more time, etiquette came to mean all the things we do to help us get along better with those we meet in our daily lives. Etiquette, or manners, guides us through all of our activities. Moreover, it lets us present ourselves with confidence and authority in all areas of our professional and personal life.

Has etiquette changed much over the years? Certain aspects of it yes, but the basic definition of it remains unaltered. Related words that were published in 1967 by Funk & Wagnalls, quoted from the book *The Emily Post Book of Etiquette From Young People* written by Elizabeth L. Post, "Believe it or not, etiquette—or good manners, if you like that phrase better—is one of those basic principles. Rules of good behavior have been built up over hundreds of years; worthless ones are continually being discarded and those proven to be useful are kept and improved upon."

Indeed, etiquette codes prescribe and restrict the ways in which people interact with each other, based on respect for other people and the accepted customs of the society. Modern etiquette codifies social interactions with others, such as: Greeting relatives, friends and acquaintances with warmth and respect; offering hospitality to guests; responding to invitations promptly; accepting gifts or favors with humility and to acknowledge them promptly with thanks (e.g., a thank-you note); refraining from insults and prying curiosity; avoiding disturbing others with unnecessary noise; contributing to conversations without dominating them; offering assistance to those in need; eating neatly and quietly; wearing clothing suited to the occasion; comforting the bereaved; following established rules of an organization upon becoming a member; arriving promptly when expected; etc.

Etiquette evolves within culture, so it is determined by culture. Conversely, etiquette also reflects and modifies culture. They have a close relationship and cannot be separated from each other. For instance, the major legacy of divinity logic we have mentioned in the above section is known as Christianity. Nowadays, many taboos in western culture are intimately connected with it. It illustrates why westerners regard 13 as an unlucky number, why they do not say God's name directly, and so on. In the following chapters you will learn more about modern etiquette and culture in western societies.

◆ Vocabulary ◆

Persian /'pɜ:ʃən/ *a.* of or relating to Iran or its people or language or culture 波斯的 *n.* a native or inhabitant of Iran 波斯人

barbarian /bɑːˈbɛəriən/ *a.* without civilizing influences 野蛮的 *n.* a member of an uncivilized people 野蛮人

Herodotus /hiˈrɔdətəs/ the ancient Greek known as the father of history; his accounts of the wars between the Greeks and Persians are the first known examples of historical writing (425 BC–485 BC) (人名) 希罗多德，古希腊历史学家

Mediterranean /ˌmeditəˈreiniən/ *a.* of or relating to or characteristic of or located near the Mediterranean Sea 地中海的

Renaissance /riˈneisns/ *n.* the period of European history at the close of the Middle Ages and the rise of the modern world; a cultural rebirth from the 14th through the middle of the 17th centuries 文艺复兴

Christianity /ˌkristʃiˈæniti/ *n.* a monotheistic system of beliefs and practices based on the Old Testament and the teachings of Jesus as embodied in the New Testament and emphasizing the role of Jesus as savior 基督教

Petri dish /ˈpiːtri ˈdiʃ/ a flat dish with a lid, used in laboratories for producing cultures of microorganisms 培养皿

anthropologist /ˌænθrəˈpɔlədʒist/ *n.* social scientist who specializes in anthropology 人类学家

archaeologist /ˌɑ:ki'ɔlədʒist/ *n.* a scientist who studies prehistoric people and their culture 考古学家

semiotic /ˌsi:mi'ɔtik/ *a.* of or relating to the study of signs and symbols as elements of communicative behavior 符号学的

assumption /ə'sʌmpʃən/ *n.* a statement that is assumed to be true and from which a conclusion can be drawn 假设

inference /'infərəns/ *n.* the act of drawing conclusions about something on the basis of information that you already have 推理，推论

syllogism /'silədʒizəm/ *n.* a kind of logical argument in which one proposition (the conclusion) is inferred from two or more others (the premises) of a certain form 三段论

premise /'premis/ *n.* a statement that is assumed to be true and from which a conclusion can be drawn 前提

proposition /ˌprɔpə'ziʃən/ *n.* (logic) a statement that affirms or denies something and is either true or false 命题

identity /ai'dentiti/ *n.* exact sameness 同一性

rationality /ˌræʃə'næliti/ *n.* the quality of being consistent with or based on logic 理性

medieval /ˌmedi'i:vəl/ *a.* relating to or belonging to the Middle Ages 中世纪的（约公元 1000 到 1450 年）

divinity /di'viniti/ *n.* the rational and systematic study of religion and its influences 神学 *a.* of the nature of religious truth 神学的

trample /'træmpl/ *v.* tread or stomp heavily or roughly 踩，踏

decree /di'kri:/ *n.* a legally binding command or decision entered on the court record 法令

codify /'kɔdi,fai/ *v.* organize into a code or system 将……编成，整理

acquaintance /ə'kweintəns/ *n.* a person with whom you are acquainted 相识的人，泛泛之交

humility /hju:'militi/ *n.* a disposition to be humble 谦恭

bereaved /bi'ri:vd/ *a.* sorrowful through loss or deprivation 丧失亲人的

◆ Exercises ◆

Ⅰ. Translation

Directions: *In this part there are 10 words or phrases in English. Please translate them into Chinese.*

1. Persian Wars   2. cultural logic   3. behavior pattern
4. Aristotle's logic   5. syllogistic   6. thought pattern
7. identity   8. divinity education   9. etiquette
10. social interaction

II. Blank filling

Directions: *In this part there is a short passage with several incomplete sentences. Please fill in all the blanks.*

The word culture has many different meanings. For anthropologists and other behavioral scientists, culture is the full range of learned human _____ patterns.

There are very likely three levels of culture that are part of your learned behavior patterns and perceptions. Most obviously, it is the body of _____ that distinguishes your specific society. The second level of culture that may be part of your identity is a _____. The third level of culture consists of _____. These are learned behavior patterns that are _____ by all of humanity collectively.

III. Essay questions

Directions: *In this part there are two essay questions. Please write the corresponding answer for each question.*

1. How did etiquette come into being?

2. What is the relationship between culture and etiquette? How does western cultural logic affect etiquette in Western societies?

Situational Dialogues

Dialogue 1

(Talking about culture shock)

Jack: Mr. Chan, you've been living in Canada for more than 3 years now. Do you feel differently about the culture now from when you first arrived?

Chan: Not really. I mean, Canada is basically as I expected. Well, perhaps a little colder.

Jack: So didn't you come up against the dreaded culture shock?

Chan: No. I was quite familiar with western culture before I left home, and I have kept an open mind about things.

Jack: So an open mind can help to prevent culture shock?

Chan: Help? It's the only way my friend! If one is prepared to learn and grow, and to appreciate different people and what they can offer, there should be no shock involved. There are always things to adjust to, but that's just part of life!

Jack: So what would you recommend for someone preparing to take a trip to China?

Chan: Read up on Chinese culture, it goes back a long way. Don't take things personally when dealing with culture shock. Keep in mind that people in a different country may have a different way of doing things. And most importantly, be willing to learn. By learning from different cultures, one can only benefit.

杰克：陈先生，你在加拿大已有 3 年多了，你觉得与你初到这儿时，文化上有什么不同吗？

陈：没有，加拿大如我期待的那样，不过就是有点冷。

杰克：那你没遇到什么可怕的文化差异吗？

陈：没有，我出国前就比较熟悉西方文化，而且我也是个没有任何偏见的人。

杰克：是否说没有偏见有助于避免因文化差异引起的不适呢？

陈：有助于？这可是唯一的方法啊！如果一个人想学习和成长，并欣赏不同的人以及他们的行为方式，就不应存在任何的冲突，应尽量改变、去适应，这就是生活的一部分。

杰克：那你对那些想去中国旅游的人有什么建议？

陈：学习中国的文化，但在遇到文化差异时别认为都是在针对你个人。要谨记，不同国家的人的处事方式会存在不同。最重要的是，抱着学习的态度。学习不同的文化，你会受益无穷。

Dialogue 2

(An interview of dealing with cultural differences)

Interviewer: Rob, you went to Brazil, didn't you?

Rob: Yes, I did.

Interviewer: So, what happened?

Rob: Well, I went into this meeting and there were about, er...seven or eight people there and I just said "Hello" to everyone and sat down. Apparently, what I should have done is to go around the room shaking hands with everyone individually. Well, you know, it's silly of me because I found out later it upset everyone. I mean, I think they felt I was taking them for granted.

Kate: Well, I know that because when I was in France the first time, I finished a meeting with "Goodbye, everyone!" to all the people in the room. There were about half a dozen people there but I was in a hurry to leave, so I just said that and left. Well, I later found out that what I should have done is shake hands with everyone in the group before leaving. Now, apparently, it's the polite thing to do.

Interviewer: Well, people shake hands in different ways, don't they?

Rob: Oh, yes, that's right, they do. See, normally I shake hands gently when I meet someone. So when I went to the US for the first time, I think people there thought my weak handshake was a sign of weakness. Apparently, people there tend to shake hands quite firmly.

Kate: Oh, gosh, you know, that reminds me: On my first trip to Germany, it was a long time ago, I was introduced to the boss in the company when he passed us in the corridor. Well, I wasn't prepared, and I mean, I had my left hand in my pocket. And when we shook hands I realized my left hand was still in my pocket. Well, that was, you know, was a very bad manners and I was quite embarrassed.

Interviewer: And how about using first names? Have you made any mistakes there?

Rob: Oh, yes, I have! When I first went to Italy I thought it was OK to use everyone's first name so as to seem friendly. And I later discovered that in business you shouldn't use someone's first name unless you are invited to. Oh, and you should always use their titles as well.

Kate: Hmm, yeah, well, when I met people in Russia, you know, they seemed to be puzzled when I shook hands with them and said "How do you do?" Well, what they do when they greet a stranger is to say their own names, so I had that all wrong!

Rob: Oh, yes, I agree with that. Remembering names is very important.

Interviewer: Shall we take a break? When we come back we'll move on to our next topic.

Kate & Rob: OK.

采访者：罗伯，你去过巴西是吗？

罗伯：是的，我去过。

采访者：发生了什么事？

罗伯：唔，我来到开会的地方，已经有七八个人在那儿了。我只是对大家说了声"你好"就坐下了。很明显，我应该这样做：环场一周然后和每个人都握手。你知道，我傻透了，因为我后来才发现大家都很生气。我是说，我想他们可能认为我无视他们的存在。

凯特：我有同感，因为我第一次去法国的时候，我对大家说了句"再见，各位！"，就结束了会议。当时大约有六个人在场，而我也急着赶路，所以说完就走了。嗯，后来我意识到，我在离开之前应该和每个人握手道别。显然，现在这是礼貌的方式。

采访者：那么，不同国家的人有不同的握手方式，是吗？

罗伯：是的，没错。一般来说，我见到某人时，会轻轻地与之握手。所以当我第一次去美国时，我想那里人一定认为我的握手很无力，这是软弱的表示。显然美国人握手都是相当有力的。

凯特：哦，天哪，你说的话让我想起了我去德国的第一次旅行。那是很久以前了，这家公司的老板突然在过道与我们相遇，于是就有人介绍我们认识。我根本没准备好，我是说我的左手插在口袋里。当我们握手时，我才意识到我的左手还在口袋里。那是非常无礼的行为，我难堪极了。

采访者：那么关于使用名字的问题，你们犯过什么错吗？

罗伯：是的，我有过。第一次去意大利时，我认为直呼名字没有问题，是友好的表示。可后来发现在商务场合，除非别人请你直呼名字，不然是不能叫别人的名字的。而且，你还得加上头衔。

凯特：对，我在俄罗斯遇见人时，就与之握手并说"你好！"可你知道，他们却看起来很困惑的样子。通常他们在遇到陌生人时会直接报出自己的名字，我完全弄错了！

罗伯：噢，我同意这一点。记住名字是很重要。

采访者：让我们休息一下吧？待会儿我们将继续下一个话题。

凯特、罗伯：好的。

Supplementary Reading

中国文化礼仪概述

What Is Best Society?
By Emily Post (1873–1960)

"SOCIETY" is an ambiguous term; it may mean much or nothing. Every human being—unless dwelling (居住) alone in a cave—is a member of society of one sort or another, and therefore it is well to define what is to be understood by the term "Best Society" and why its authority is recognized. Best Society abroad is always the oldest aristocracy (贵族); composed not so much of persons of title, which may be new, as of those families and communities which have for the longest period of time known highest cultivation. Our own Best Society is represented by social groups which have had, since this is America, widest rather than longest association with old world cultivation. Cultivation is always the basic attribute of Best Society, much as we hear in this country of an "aristocracy of wealth."

To the general public a long purse is synonymous (同义的) with high position—a theory dear to the heart of the "yellow" press and eagerly fostered in the preposterous (可笑的) social functions of screen drama. It is true that Best Society is comparatively rich; it is true that the hostess of great wealth, who constantly and lavishly entertains, will shine, at least to the readers of the press, more brilliantly than her less affluent (富裕的) sister. Yet the latter, through her quality of birth, her poise (优雅的姿态), her inimitable (独特的) distinction, is often the jewel of deeper water in the social crown of her time.

The most advertised commodity is not always intrinsically (本质上地) the best, but is sometimes merely the product of a company with plenty of money to spend on advertising. In the same way, money brings certain people before the public—sometimes they are persons of "quality," quite as often the so-called "society leaders" featured in the public press do not belong to good society at all, in spite of their many published photographs and the energies of their press-agents. Or possibly they do belong to "smart" society; but if too much advertised, instead of being the "queens" they seem, they might more accurately be classified as the court jesters (弄臣，小丑) of today.

The Imitation and the Genuine

New York, more than any city in the world, unless it be Paris, loves to be amused, thrilled, and surprised all at the same time; and will accept with outstretched (张开的) hands anyone who can perform this astounding (令人震惊的) feat (技艺). Do not underestimate the ability that one can achieve it: A scintillating (妙趣横生的) wit, an arresting (引人注意的) originality, a talent for entertaining that amounts to genius, and gold poured literally like rain, are the least requirements.

Puritan (清教徒的) America on the other hand demanding, as a ticket of admission to her Best Society, the qualifications of birth, manners and cultivation, clasps her hands tight across her slim trim waist and announces severely that New York's "Best" is, in her opinion, very "bad" indeed. But this is because Puritan America, as well as the general public, mistakes the jester for the queen.

As a matter of fact, Best Society is not at all like a court with an especial queen or king, nor is it confined to any one place or group, but might better be described as an unlimited brotherhood which spreads over the entire surface of the globe, the members of which are invariably (总是) people of cultivation and worldly knowledge, who have not only perfect manners but a perfect manner. Manners are made up of trivialities (琐事) of deportment (举止) which can be easily learned if one does not happen to know them; manner is personality—the outward manifestation of one's innate (天生的) character and attitude toward life. A gentleman, for instance, will never be ostentatious (夸耀的) or overbearing (专横的) any more than he will ever be servile (奴性的), because these attributes never animate (激励) the impulses of a well-bred person. A man whose manners suggest the grotesque (怪诞的) is invariably a person of imitation rather than of real position.

Etiquette must, if it is to be of more than trifling use, include ethics as well as manners. Certainly what one is, is of far greater importance than what one appears to be. A knowledge of etiquette is of course essential to one's decent behavior, just as clothing is essential to one's decent appearance; and precisely as one wears the latter without being self-conscious of having on shoes and perhaps gloves, one who has good manners is equally unself-conscious in the observance of etiquette, the precepts (箴言) of which must be so thoroughly absorbed as to make their observance a matter of instinct rather than of conscious obedience.

Thus Best Society is not a fellowship of the wealthy, nor does it seek to exclude those who are not of exalted (地位高的) birth; but it is an association of gentle-folk, of which good form in speech, charm of manner, knowledge of the social amenities (礼节), and instinctive consideration for the feelings of others, are the credentials (证明书) by which society the world over recognizes its chosen members.

Chapter 2
Etiquette of Greetings

见面礼仪

在本章中，你将了解到：
- 西方的称谓语
- 打招呼的方式
- 介绍的礼节
- 道别的方式
- 握手、吻礼和拥抱的场合与礼仪

Intensive Reading

2.1 Forms of Address

Forms of address are words and phrases used for addressing. They refer to the collocutor and thus contain a strong element of deixis. In most western languages, forms of address concentrate on three word classes: pronoun, verb, and noun. These are supplemented by words which are synthetically dependent on them.

Pronouns of address are pronouns referring to the collocutor(s). These are, above all, second person pronouns, such as English *you*. Other grammatical persons can also act as pronouns of address if only they refer to the communication partner.

Verb forms of address are verbs in which reference to the collocutor is expressed, e.g., by means of inflectional suffixes. Frequently such verb forms are redundant, that is, they are accompanied by a pronoun of address. For instance, in Finnish "Mihin menet?" means "Where do you go?"

Nouns of address are substantives and adjectives which designate collocutors or refer to them in some way. This class comprises the most diverse types, some of which shall here be mentioned because of their frequency.

(i) Names. Using first name is widespread, especially in the United States. Americans of all ages may prefer to be called by their first names. In their opinions, addressing people by their first names usually indicates friendliness.

(ii) Kinship term (KT). These are terms for blood relations or for affines. When a KT is used for addressing someone who is not related to the speaking in one way or another, this is called a fictive use of a KT. For example, in England, a child may call a female friend of their parents "Aunty Kay."

(iii) General forms. In addition to Mr., Mrs., and Miss, there is one more term, Ms. Ms. is used neither for a married or unmarried woman. In the UK and USA, "Ms." is merely a replacement for "Miss." Be sure that the four terms, Mr., Mrs., Miss and Ms., are followed by the last names. Apart from the four terms, you can always use "sir" or "madam" when you first meet someone and want to be respectful. And they are not followed by either the first names or the last names.

(iv) Titles. These terms are usually bestowed, achieved by appointment (such as Doctor,

General, Senator, Bishop), or are inherited (such as Duke, Count). Most of these titles are followed by surnames, e.g., Judge Clark. But for a university professor, you may call him professor, with or without his surname.

(v) Abstract nouns. These forms of address originally referred to some abstract quality of the addressee, e.g., (Your) Excellency, (Your) Honor, (Your) Grace.

2.2 Ways of Daily Greetings

There are two types of daily greetings according to the degree of formality. One is formal, such as "Good morning," "Good afternoon," "Good evening," and "Goodbye." These greetings are always accompanied by general forms or formal titles (see the above section). The other is informal, such as "Hello," "Hi," "Goodbye," "Bye," "Bye-bye," and "See you." It is worth noting that "Good morning" is still widely used in daily life, while "Good afternoon/Good evening" gives way to "Hello" or "Hi." In informal occasions, the use of first names is fairly common, especially in the United States. Of course, not only in the United States, the days in Britain when men referred to or introduced each other by their surnames, and when office hierarchies were constantly marked by the use of the prefix "Mr." or "Miss" are long gone. Informality is the order of the day and first names are becoming popular; even in professional situations, when dealing with doctors, lawyers, policemen, and bank managers, informality is being adopted.

One more point about greetings. In some places and certain occasions, people also smile and greet to strangers. For instance, when in a confined place or an occasion of face-to-face confrontation, it is polite to greet someone you don't know rather than to avert your eyes from them deliberately. Otherwise, you will be regarded as rude and disrespectful.

2.3 Courtesy of Introduction

If you are the link between people who have never met, it is up to you to make the introductions. There are several rules concerning hierarchy of introduction: (i) men should be introduced to women first; (ii) younger people should be introduced to elder people first; (iii) lower ranks should be introduced to higher ranks first; (iv) individuals should be introduced to the group first and then the group to the individual. For example, "Everyone, this is Mary. Mary, this is Jim, Bob and Sue."

Unless the occasion is formal there's no need to mention surnames. If possible, offering a little information about each person as you introduce them like, "Robert and I were at school together," will help to break the ice.

"How do you do?" is the traditional British greeting in introduction, which is seldom used in America. The appropriate response is to reiterate the phrase "How do you do?" In situations where this exchange may seem too formal, a friendly "Hello" will usually do.

At an even more informal level, if someone says "Hi, how are you?" or "Hi, how's things?" The response should be positive and upbeat: "Fine, thanks, and you?"" or "Fine, thanks, càn't complain."

When people are introduced to each other, non-verbal language such as a handshake is always adopted to show respect and politeness, especially in business occasions.

2.4 Ways of Saying Goodbye

Normally, people won't make a departure without saying goodbye after a chat. It is easy to say goodbye, but do you know the right way to bid farewell in western societies? The person, ending the encounter whether on the phone, leaving the room or responding to a text-messaging, is responsible to let the other party know that they are ending the communication. This is not only proper, but also considerate. Interestingly, a western guest who wants to end a visit always says something from his/her own point of view rather than for the sake of the host, for example, "I'm afraid I stayed too long." or "It's about time I made a move. I have to get up early tomorrow." More politely, they will express gratefulness while saying goodbye like, "I really enjoyed talking with you." or "Thank you for your wonderful party. I enjoyed myself very much." Sometimes, they will say, "I hope to see you again very soon." or "I will contact you." which are merely farewell words.

As the host and/or hostess, it is typical for them to respect the guest's will without urging him/her to stay or accompanying him/her a long way outside the door.

2.5 Handshaking, Social Kissing and Hugging

2.5.1 Handshaking

Handshaking is a widely adopted practice which originated from ancient Greece as far back as the 5th century BC. The handshake is initiated when the two hands touch, immediately. It is commonly done upon meeting, greeting, parting, offering congratulations, expressing gratitude, or completing an agreement. In sports or other competitive activities, it is also done as a sign of good sportsmanship. Its purpose is to convey trust, balance, and equality.

Unless health issues or local customs dictate, otherwise a handshake should always be made using bare hands. In some regions especially in Continental Europe, attempting to perform a handshake while wearing gloves may be seen as an inappropriate or even derogatory behavior. However, the requirement to remove a glove depends. A gentleman should never shake hands with a lady without first removing his right glove, while if a lady wears opera gloves (see Chapter 7 for details), it is unnecessary to remove them.

In Anglophone countries, shaking hands is considered as the standard greeting in business situations. In casual non-business situations, men are more likely to shake hands than women.

There are some conventions about handshaking. When two men or two women meet, it is usually the older who should first hold out his/her hand. When a man and a woman meet, it is the woman who should first offer her hand. When two persons of different ranks meet, it is the one with higher rank who should first offer his/her hand.

How do you shake hands with others in a correct way? Actually, it is not as simple a question as you might think. First, keep eye contact with the person you are going to shake your hands with. Second, smile and say "Hello" as you extend your right arm and right hand forward. Third, apply pressure to the other person's hand. Last, once both your hands are clasped, move it up and down once or twice. Maintain eye contact and smile during the time.

2.5.2 Social Kissing

Cheek kissing is most common in Europe and Latin America and has become a standard greeting in Southern Europe. It is also becoming increasingly popular in Britain, but it is by no means an accepted norm, and is therefore a potential minefield.

To kiss or not to kiss? This is usually dependent on situation, age, background, profession, and your relationship. As a general rule, don't kiss people you don't know. Don't kiss colleagues. Do kiss close friends and dates. The key is to make your actions clear to avoid embarrassing confusion.

While cheek kissing is a common greeting in many cultures, each country has a unique way of kissing. In Russia, Slovenia, the Netherlands and other countries it is customary to "kiss three times, on alternate cheeks." Italians and Hungarians usually kiss twice in a greeting, and in Mexico and Belgium only one kiss is necessary. Usually it's right cheek first. You should pull back decisively (but don't be too abrupt) if you are just giving one kiss.

Social Kissing

How to kiss others on the cheek? Cheek skin must make brief, light contact; sound effects and saliva traces are to be avoided at all cost. It is considered insincere just holding cheek against cheek and air kissing with "mwah, mwah" side effects has become synonymous with shallowness. If you'd prefer to shake hands, be sure to hold your hands out before any kissing movements begin. But, if you're part of a group introduction, don't be the only non-kisser at the party.

2.5.3 Hugging

Hugs are an important expression of affection. By hugging someone, you remind them that you care about them and support them. Hugs are easy but it is not always easy to give. To hug you need to be friends or more, then smile at the person and hug them. If it is with someone of the opposite gender, you have to be in a very good relationship. Just take it slow and steady.

First, approach the person. Depending on the person's relationship to you, you might approach differently.

Second, embrace. Lean forward and wrap your arms around the person.

Third, don't hug too tightly. The best way to judge how tightly or loosely to hug is to let whomever you're hugging indicate what they want by how hard they squeeze. If they are soft, be soft back; if they like bear hugs and squeeze tightly, hug back the same way (but don't make him/her hard to breathe).

Fourth, don't let go too early. A hug is a powerful way to communicate your caring for another person, as it can greatly improve one's mood. If someone hugs you, they may want a long, loving hug (maybe they are upset or down), so just go along with it and hug them until they let go or loosen their hold. If you try to end it early, it may seem awkward for both of you.

A good approach no matter what your relationship with the person you'll be hugging is to walk up to him or her from a few (maybe three) feet away, arms open. When you get to them, wrap your arms around their body. Hold for a few seconds, and then let go.

◆ Vocabulary ◆

deixis /'daiksis/ *n.* the function of pointing or specifying from the perspective of a participant in an act of speech or writing 指示语

synthetically /sin'θetikəli/ *ad.* in a synthetic manner 综合地

collocutor /'kɔləˌkju:tə/ *n.* a person who talks or engages in conversation with another 谈话者

inflectional /in'flekʃənəl/ *a.* expressing grammatical relations by means of affixes or changes in vowels or consonants（语法）屈折的

suffix /'sʌfiks/ *n.* an affix that is added at the end of the word 后缀

redundant /ri'dʌndənt/ *a.* more than is needed, desired, or required 冗余的

substantive /'sʌbstəntiv/ *n.* a noun or a pronoun that is used in place of a noun 名词

designate /'dezigneit/ *v.* assign a name or title to 指明

kinship /'kinˌʃip/ *n.* state of relatedness or connection by blood or marriage or adoption 亲属关系

affine /ə'fain/ *n.* kin by marriage 姻亲

fictive /'fiktiv/ *a.* of, relating to, or able to engage in imaginative invention; not genuine 假想的, 非真实的

bestow /bi'stəu/ *v.* present 授予

inherit /in'herit/ *v.* receive from a predecessor 继承

courtesy /'kə:tisi/ *n.* a courteous manner 礼貌

hierarchy /'haiərɑ:ki/ *n.* a series of ordered groupings of people or things within a system 层级; 等级制度

confined /kən'faind/ *a.* enclosed by a confining fence（指空间）有限的

avert /ə'və:t/ *v.* to turn away or aside (as the eyes) in avoidance 转移，避开

reiterate /ri:'itə,reit/ *v.* to state or do over again or repeatedly sometimes with wearying effect 反复地说

upbeat /'ʌpbi:t/ *a.* cheerful, optimistic 乐观的

derogatory /di'rɔgə,təri/ *a.* expressive of a low opinion 不敬的

Anglophone /'æŋgləufəun/ *a.* consisting of or belonging to an English-speaking population especially in a country where two or more languages are spoken 以英语为母语者

saliva /sə'laivə/ *n.* slightly alkaline secretion of water, mucin, protein, salts, and often a starch-splitting enzyme (as ptyalin) that is secreted into the mouth by salivary glands, lubricates ingested food, and often begins the breakdown of starches 唾液

◆ Exercises ◆

Ⅰ.Translation

Directions: *In this part there are 10 words or phrases in English. Please translate them into Chinese.*

1. form of address
2. general form
3. kinship term
4. fictive use of KT
5. title
6. face-to-face confrontation
7. surname
8. eye contact
9. handshake
10. cheek kissing

Ⅱ. Blank filling

Directions: *In this part there is a short passage with several incomplete sentences. Please fill in all the blanks.*

In most western languages, forms of address concentrate on three word classes: _____, verb, _____. Among them, nouns of address comprises the most diverse types, including names, _____ like "uncle," general forms like "_____," _____ like "doctor," abstract nouns like "Your Excellency," etc.,

Ⅲ. Essay questions

Directions: *In this part there are two essay questions. Please write the corresponding answer for each question.*

1.　Suppose you are at a party with your younger cousin (Susan Wang, female). Suddenly you see one of your colleagues (Bob Jones, male) coming towards you, who is older than you. How will you introduce them?

2.　What are the most common greeting gestures in western countries? How are they applied in daily greetings?

Situational Dialogues

Dialogue 1

(Bumping into an old friend)

Fred: Hey, aren't you Ted Williams?

Ted: Yes, that's right.

Fred: I thought so. I'm Fred Miller. Remember? We were in Class 3 at college together.

Ted: Well, how about that! It's great to see you again, Fred. You haven't changed a bit.

Fred: Oh, I don't know about that. 20 years is a long time. But, tell me, what have you been up to?

Ted: I've been running a bookstore passed on to me by my father.

Fred: Oh, really? I remember you were very fond of music in college.

Ted: Yes, but I gave it up 10 years ago.

弗雷德：嗨，这不是泰德·威廉姆斯吗？

泰德：是的。

弗雷德：我认为是。我是弗雷德·米勒。记得吗？我们上大学时同在 3 班。

泰德：想起来了，弗雷德，见到你真高兴。你一点都没变。

弗雷德：噢，我也不太清楚，毕竟 20 年还是很长一段时间。告诉我，你一直在做什么？

泰德：我一直在经营我父亲传给我的书店。

弗雷德：噢，真的？我记得你上大学时很喜欢音乐。

泰德：是的，但 10 年前我就放弃了。

Dialogue 2

(Seeing a friend off)

Jones: It's really very kind of you to come to see me off, Mr. Zhang.

Zhang: Not at all. Mr. Jones, I'm sorry you're unable to stay in Lanzhou a little while longer.

Jones: Me, too. I'm very grateful to you for your warm hospitality.

Zhang: It was nothing at all. What's your flight number?

Jones: It's Flight No.104, Northwest Orient Airlines. My plane is scheduled to take off at 2:30 pm.

Zhang: Then you still have a couple of hours to kill. How about having some refreshments in this coffee shop?

Jones: That would be nice.

(They enter the coffee shop at the airport.)

Zhang: What would you like to have, Mr. Jones?

Jones: Coffee, please.

Zhang: And how about something to eat?

Jones: No, thanks. I had a very late breakfast. Just coffee will do.

Zhang: All right. Oh, waitress. Two coffees, please.

Waitress: Yes, sir. Anything else?

Zhang: No, thanks.

Waitress: All right. Please wait a moment.

Jones: Oh, I think they're announcing my flignt over the public address system. I'd better be going.

Zhang: Bon voyage, Mr. Jones.

Jones: Goodbye, Mr. Zhang, I'll contact you again.

Zhang: Goodbye.

琼斯：张先生，您专程来送我真是太客气了。

张：哪里，哪里。琼斯先生，您不能在兰州多住一段时间我感到很遗憾。

琼斯：甚是遗憾。您如此盛情招待我，真是太感激了。

张：没什么的。您的班机号码是几号？

琼斯：是西北航空公司的 104 号班机。我的班机预定在下午两点三十分起飞。

张：那您还有一两个小时可以打发。我们到这家咖啡屋里喝点东西好吗？

琼斯：好呀！

(他们走进了机场咖啡屋。)

张：琼斯先生，你要来些什么？

琼斯：请给我一杯咖啡。

张：要不要来一些吃的？

琼斯：不用了，谢谢。我早餐吃得很晚，咖啡就足够了。

张：好的。服务员，请给我们两杯咖啡。

服务员：好的，先生。还要些其他的吗？

张：不用了，谢谢。

服务员：好的，请稍候。

琼斯：哦，我听到扩音器在广播我的班机了。我该走了。

张：琼斯先生，祝您一路顺风。

琼斯：再见了，张先生，我会再跟你联络的。

Dialogue 3

(Introduction)

Mary: David, I would like to introduce my teacher, Miss Smith, to you. Shall we go and meet her now?

David: Okay. Let's go.

Mary: Miss Smith, this is my friend David. David, this is my teacher, Miss Smith.

Smith: How do you do, David?

David: How do you do, Miss Smith? I'm glad to meet you.

Smith: I'm glad to meet you, too. Are you and Mary in the same class?

David: No. I'm in Mr. Brown's class.

Mary: Miss Smith, David is a very good soccer player. He has played soccer for years.

Smith: Has he? I like watching soccer games.

David: Will you come and watch us play some day, Miss Smith?

Smith: Yes, I will. Thank you.

(The bell rings.)

Mary: We must go to class now. Goodbye, Miss Smith.

Smith: Goodbye, Mary. Goodbye, David.

David: Goodbye.

玛丽：戴维，我想把我的老师，史密斯小姐介绍给你，我们现在去见她，好吗？

戴维：好的，我们走吧。

玛丽：史密斯小姐，这是我的朋友戴维。戴维，这是我的老师，史密斯小姐。

史密斯：你好，戴维。

戴维：你好，史密斯小姐。认识你很高兴。

史密斯：认识你，我也很高兴。你和玛丽在一班吗？

戴维：不，我在布朗先生的那个班。

玛丽：史密斯小姐，戴维是个很好的足球运动员，他踢足球有许多年了。

史密斯：是吗？我喜欢看足球比赛。

戴维：哪天你来看我们踢足球好吗，史密斯小姐？

史密斯：好的，我一定去，谢谢你。

(铃响了。)

玛丽：我们得去上课了，再见，史密斯小姐。

史密斯：再见，玛丽。再见，戴维。

戴维：再见。

Supplementary Reading

中国社交称谓

Eye Contact

By Luke Jackson

"Are you listening to me?" "Look at me when I am talking to you." As kids, how familiar are those words? Don't they just make you groan? (And that's putting it politely!) Adults seem to make a really big deal of getting people to look at them when they are talking. Apparently it is seen as rude if you don't look at least in the direction of the speaker. This world is full of so many stupid rules! I really hate this one.

[My brother] Joseph rarely looks at anyone when they are talking to him and part of the work they do at school is to get him to do so. I can see the reason why they do this with Joe because he has a big listening and attention problem. When he is not looking at someone he is usually doing his own thing and people are wasting their time talking to him. To find out whether your child or the person you are working with or talking to is listening, the easiest way is to ask them a question related to what you have just said. If they answer and are obviously listening, then personally I think it is irrelevant whether they are looking at you or not.

When I look someone straight in the eye, particularly someone I am not familiar with, the feeling is so uncomfortable that I cannot really describe it. First of all I feel as if their eyes are burning me and I really feel as if I am looking into the face of an alien. I know this sounds rude but I am telling it how it is. If I get past that stage and don't look away, then whilst someone is talking I find myself staring really hard and looking at their features and completely forgetting to listen to what they are saying. Mum says when I was little I used to go right up to people and stare in their faces. They probably looked funny—I often have to stop myself from giggling (咯咯地笑) when I examine people's faces; there are some very strange ones around!

Sometimes it is too hard to concentrate on listening and looking at the same time. People are hard enough to understand as their words are often so very cryptic (含义隐晦的), but when their faces are moving around, their eyebrows rising and falling and their eyes getting wider then squinting, I cannot fathom (理解) all that out in one go, so to be honest I don't even try.

As kids, I have found a compromise (妥协，折衷) to this problem that I am practising and working well on. I look at people's mouths. That means that the other person is satisfied enough because you are looking in their direction but yet you do not have to have that horrendous (可怕的), burning into your very soul feeling that comes with staring into someone's eyes. Just try looking hard at someone's mouth when they are talking and see how many shapes it makes. The trouble with this is the temptation (诱惑) to amuse yourself with this and forget to listen. Another good

ploy (策略) is to look in the direction of the speaker's ear. This is a good one because it reminds you to listen and provides no distractions (unless of course you find someone with a wiggly [扭动的] one!).

It is best to find some kind of compromise so that you don't stand out too much and appear rude. It can be done. Remember, there is more than one way to skin a cat! (Mum told me this one—I think it sounds horrible.)

Chapter 3
Etiquette of Interpersonal Communication

人际交往礼仪

在本章中，你将了解到：
- 女士优先的传统
- 应邀做客时应注意些什么
- 赠礼收礼的礼仪
- 打电话的礼仪
- 西方人使用最频繁的礼貌用语

Intensive Reading

3.1 Ladies First

The "ladies first" rule is a very old tradition. According to Judaism and the Torah, the story goes that when Moses was instructed to inform the people of Israel about the Torah, he was told to "speak to the house of Jacob, and tell the sons of Israel." Since the house of Jacob appears first in the instructions, and it refers to women, the theory follows that Moses had to speak first with the ladies. This is probably the origin of the phrase "ladies first."

In Europe as well as in the United States, you will usually see men open doors for women, help women on and off their coats, and pull table chairs for women before and after dinner. Women generally walk ahead of men into a room or a restaurant, unless the men have to be ahead of the ladies to choose the table, to open the door or a car, to lead them downstairs, or render other services. On the street, men just about walk or cross the street on the side of ladies which is closer to the traffic.

At parties, the host usually shows the guest upon his arrival at the sitting room. If the guest is a lady, most men in the room will stand up when she comes in. The ladies in the sitting room will not stand up whether the new comer is a man or a woman. Women of all ages still appreciate this courtesy, although the custom is followed by fewer people now than in the past, especially with the younger generation.

3.2 Paying a Visit

When you are invited to someone's home, by all means accept their invitation if you are available. But if you are busy, do not be afraid to decline the invitation, and perhaps suggest a time that would be better. Your host should not feel insulted.

Sometimes a friend from the West might have invited you to drop in by anytime. But it is best to call before visiting to make sure it is convenient for them. Do not pay a visit without making an appointment in advance, unless you are very close friends or relatives.

If you are willing to accept an invitation, you must make it a point to inquire about the day of the week, the date, the time, and the place. If you don't know the way to the place, be sure to ask for instructions.

If you later find that you cannot attend, you should telephone the host and explain why you cannot make it. You should inform your host as far ahead of time as possible, because she may wish to invite someone else in your place.

If you have accepted the invitation, you should get to the place at the fixed time, or even ten minutes after that. If you happen to be earlier than expected, you had better wait, because your hostess might be busy doing other things and not be ready to meet you earlier. If you are likely to be 15 minutes late, please make a telephone call to your hostess. Of course, you must have a proper reason for being late.

Upon your arrival, you may present some flowers to your host. But it is not necessary to do so, except on some special occasions, such as birthdays, Christmas, New Years, and so on. If you are going to stay overnight, it is customary to bring the hostess a small present, often a book, a box of candy, a bottle of wine, or some other similar gift.

If something is offered by the host, being frank and direct may bring comfort for both the guest and the host. For instance, you have drunk enough coffee when your western friend is about to refill your cup again. Instead of accepting his offer with reluctance, you may say to him frankly "No, thank you." It won't hurt anyone's feelings.

If you intend to do something that might have an effect on the people around, e.g., lighting a cigarette, remember to ask for permission.

Whenever you have been a guest in a home, you should definitely send a hand-written thank-you note as soon as possible. Make the note sound as if you were talking to your hostess in person. Thank-you notes are also written for a gift, a favor or some other hospitality. For details of thank-you notes, refer to Chapter 4.

3.3 Giving and Receiving Gifts

There are lots of occasions calling for giving gifts: Bridal showers, weddings, baby showers, birthdays, house warming parties, visiting one's home, visiting a patient, funerals, etc. When westerners give gifts in formal occasions (such as a birthday, a wedding, Christmas), a card is always attached to the gift, which is used to congratulate the receiver as well as make themselves known by the receiver.

The gifts are always elaborately wrapped. In formal occasions wrapping is especially important. While in casual occasions (such as a house warming party or visiting one's home), wrapping is less important.

When presenting gift, a westerner will tell the receiver how careful he or she picked the gift and it is a wonderful one. It shows that he or she really cares about the receiver. Do not be too modest about the gift you pick, otherwise your western friend is likely to feel you do think little of his or her friendship.

Avoid giving too expensive or too personal gifts to the receiver unless you are very close. Generally speaking, cash, fine jewelry, medicine, nutritional supplements, advertised goods, and fruit are not common choices for giving gifts.

If you are invited to someone's home, it is standard practice to bring wine/champagne, flowers, and chocolates for your hosts. Sprits, on the other hand, are a matter of personal taste and best not given as a present. The usual European caveats apply when giving flowers: No red roses, white lilies, or chrysanthemums.

When a gift is received, open it at the presence of the giver. Receiving cards follow the same procedure. Show your gratitude and appreciation to the giver at the same time beyond a simple thank-you. If possible, ask the giver relevant questions about the present, or tell him/her when you will use it. Disappointment, distaste, or just indifference must be hidden at all costs. For all but the most casually given gifts, a written thank-you note is appropriate soon afterwards.

3.4 Phone Calling Etiquette

If you want to make a phone call, choose the right time, neither too early in the morning nor too late in the evening. When making a call, identify yourself immediately. Do not make them guess who is calling. Then ask them if it's convenient to talk now. Talk loud enough directly into the phone to be heard—without shouting. If they have to be put on hold, ask if you can call them back rather than keep them waiting indefinitely on the line. If you have dialed a wrong number, apologize. Don't just hang up.

Here are some useful expressions of **making a call**:

● Hello, this is Rita (speaking). May I speak to John?
● Hello? Get Jack to the phone, please.
● I'd like to speak to Mr. Doner.
● Could I talk to your manager, please?
● May I have the pleasure of addressing Mr. White?
● Can you give me his office extension number?
● How can I reach him by phone?
● Could you ask her to call me?
● Please have him return my call.
● I can phone again later.
● Would you tell him I rang?
● Could I leave a message?

If you are going to receive a call, answer your phone promptly to save them having to ring again and greet the caller pleasantly. In a multinational corporation, the phone must be picked up after the second ring. When receiving a business telephone, you should answer with the company's name first instead of saying "Hello," for instance, "Tiger Electronics. Good morning!"

If you have company, let the caller know that you must be brief or that you will call back later.

If the person wanted on the phone isn't available, take messages for him or her clearly and politely. If it is necessary to transfer the call, first tell the caller that you are transferring the call and then do it. Always let the caller be the one to end the call first.

Here are some useful expressions of **receiving a call**:

- Hello? Peter's residence.
- Hold on for a moment, please.
- Hold the line, please. I'll fetch him up.
- Hello? This is John. Who's speaking?
- He is not available right now.
- He is on another line.
- Sorry, but he is out.
- Any message for him?
- Can I take a message?
- Do you want to leave word for him to call you?
- Would you like to leave a message?
- Could you ring again in 30 minutes, please?

3.5 Four Dynamic Terms of Courtesy

There are four terms of courtesy which are most frequently used in western societies. These terms are so dynamic in daily life that it is probably beyond your imagination. They are even taught once a toddler starts learning to speak. With the magic words, life seems to be in less conflict and more harmony. Guess what the four terms are? Yes, they are "Please," "Thank you," "Sorry," and "Excuse me."

How are the four terms used correctly? First, if you have to trouble others to help you, "please" is a must to say. In an imperative sentence, once "please" is used, the tone would be more polite and pleasant. Others will be willing to do a favor for you. In answer to a "thank you," you may say "It's my pleasure," "Don't mention it," etc.

Second, whenever others do something for you, you should always show your gratitude by saying "Thank you." No matter whom they are, a waiter, a colleague, or even your parents, a sincere "thank you" will make them feel warm and think you are not taking them for granted.

Third, there are many occasions to use the term, "Sorry." If you offend someone indeliberately, a "sorry" will ease the tension. If you have to refuse someone's good intention or say something that sounds disagreeable to them, a "sorry" will make them feel less uncomfortable. For example, "I'm sorry, but I won't be able to come tonight."

Last, similar to "Sorry," "Excuse me," is another frequently used term to express one's apology. If you try to draw someone's attention, you would say "Excuse me;" if you have to interrupt someone's words, you would say "Excuse me;" if you walk through the crowd and want someone to give way to you, you would say "Excuse me;" if you disturb others with unnecessary noise in public, such as coughing, burping, yawning, or sneezing, an "Excuse me" is a must.

◆ Vocabulary ◆

Judaism /ˈdʒuːdeiizəm/ **n.** a religion developed among the ancient Hebrews and characterized by belief in one transcendent God who has revealed himself to Abraham, Moses, and the Hebrew prophets and by a religious life in accordance with Scriptures and rabbinic traditions 犹太教

Torah /ˈtɔrə/ **n.** the scroll of parchment on which the first five books of the Hebrew Scripture is written 律法，圣经旧约之首五卷

Moses /ˈməuziz/ **n.** a religious leader, lawgiver and prophet, to whom the authorship of the Torah is traditionally attributed （人名）摩西，《圣经》古以色列人首领

Israel /ˈizriːəl/ **n.** kingdom in ancient Palestine comprising the lands occupied by the Hebrew people; established about 1025 BC; divided about 933 BC into a S kingdom (Judah) & a N kingdom (Israel) 以色列

cigarette /ˌsigəˈret/ **n.** finely ground tobacco wrapped in paper 香烟

hospitality /ˌhɔspiˈtæliti/ **n.** kindness in welcoming guests or strangers 好意

elaborately /iˈlæbərətli/ **ad.** with elaboration 精致地

wrap /ræp/ **v.** arrange or fold as a cover or protection 包装

champagne /ʃæmˈpein/ **n.** a white sparkling wine either produced in Champagne or resembling that produced there 香槟

spirit /ˈspirit/ **n.** distilled rather than fermented liquor, usually in plural form （复）烈酒

caveat /ˈkæviˌæt/ **n.** warning against certain acts 告诫

chrysanthemum /kriˈsænθəməm/ **n.** the flower of a chrysanthemum plant 菊花

gratitude /ˈgrætitjuːd/ **n.** a feeling of thankfulness and appreciation 感谢

distaste /disˈteist/ **n.** a feeling of intense dislike 不喜欢

extension /iksˈtenʃən/ **n.** an additional telephone set that is connected to the same telephone line 分机

promptly /ˈprɔmptli/ **ad.** with little or no delay 迅速地

transfer /trænsˈfəː/ **v.** to cause to pass from one to another 转接

toddler /ˈtɔdlə/ **n.** a young child who has only just learned to walk or who still walks unsteadily with small, quick steps 蹒跚学步的孩童

indeliberately /indiˈlibəritli/ **adv.** without intention 不是故意地，无心地

◆ Exercises ◆

Ⅰ. Translation

Directions: *In this part there are 10 words or phrases in English. Please translate them into Chinese.*

1. ladies first
2. render services
3. decline an invitation
4. make an appointment
5. thank-you note
6. house warming party
7. extension number
8. leave a message
9. hold the line
10. do a favor

Ⅱ. Blank filling

Directions: *In this part there is a short passage with several incomplete sentences. Please fill in all the blanks.*

The four terms of courtesy which are most frequently used in western societies are "_____," "_____," "_____," and "_____." In an imperative sentence, once "_____" is used, the tone would be more polite and pleasant. Whenever others do something for you, you should always show your gratitude by saying "_____." "_____" and "_____" are frequently used terms to express one's apology. For instance, if you have to refuse someone's good intention, or say something that sounds disagreeable to them, a "_____" will make them feel less uncomfortable. And if you disturb others with unnecessary noise in public, such as coughing, _____, yawning or _____, you should say "_____."

Ⅲ. Essay questions

Directions: *In this part there are two essay questions. Please write the corresponding answer for each question.*

1. How do good-mannered men in the West behave when they are with women? On what occasions should they walk ahead of women? On what occasions should they go behind women?

2. Suppose an American friend of yours, Lily, is giving a birthday gift to you. What would you do upon receiving it? And how will you express your gratitude to her afterwards?

Situational Dialogues

Dialogue 1

(Paying a visit at somebody's home)

Ken: Hello, Rob.

Rob: Hello, Ken. Hello Barbara. Come in. Can I take your coats?

Ken: Thank you very much. What a lovely house!

Rob: I'm glad you like it.

Ken: Where's Anna?

Rob: Oh, she's in the kitchen. She'll be here in a minute. Just go into the dining room. How about a
    drink before dinner?

Ken: That's a good idea.

Anna: Here we are. Dinner's ready. Sit down, everybody.

Barbara: Thank you very much, Anna. Everything looks wonderful and it smells delicious too.

Anna: I'll put the salad in the middle of the table. Shall I serve you?

Barbara: No, it's all right. We can help ourselves.

Anna: Rob, would you pour the wine, please? Ken, help yourself to some vegetables, too.

Rob: Would you like some more brandy, Barbara?

Barbara: Oh, no, thanks. No more for me. I'm driving tonight.

Rob: Oh, come on, just a little.

Barbara: No, really... I mustn't. Let me help you with the washing-up.

Rob: The washing-up? No, no, don't worry. We always leave that until the next morning.

肯：你好，罗伯。

罗伯：你好，肯。你好，芭芭拉，快进来，把大衣给我。

肯：谢谢，多漂亮的房子！

罗伯：你喜欢我很高兴。

肯：安娜呢？

罗伯：她在厨房，马上就过来，咱们去餐厅吧。饭前来点喝的怎么样？

肯：好主意。

安娜：好了，饭好了。大家请坐。

芭芭拉：非常谢谢你，安娜。每道菜看上去都不错，而且闻着也很香。

安娜：我把沙拉放在桌子中间，需要我给你夹点吗？

芭芭拉：不用了，我们自己来。

安娜：罗伯，倒点酒好吗？肯，自己多夹点蔬菜。

罗伯：芭芭拉，再来点白兰地吗？

芭芭拉：哦，不了，谢谢。不要了。我今晚开车。

罗伯：哦，来吧，再来一点。

芭芭拉：不要了，真的，一点也不要。让我帮你洗碗吧。

罗伯：洗碗？不，不，不用管。我们总是第二天早晨才去洗。

Dialogue 2

(Buying somebody a gift)

Bill: I'm thinking of buying something for my friend. Could you give me some advice?

Liu: Sure. What would you like to buy?

Bill: I'd like to buy some typical Chinese products.

Liu: Then you can buy some Chinese silk products, such as embroidered handkerchiefs, tablecloths or blouses.

Bill: That's a good idea! Where can I buy them?

Liu: I suggest the First Department Store on Silver Street. It's only two blocks away from here.

Bill: Are the things very expensive there?

Liu: No. The prices are very reasonable in the First Department Store.

Bill: Great. Thanks a lot.

Liu: You're welcome.

(Later, in the Department Store)

Salesman: How do you like this silk scarf? It is a typical Chinese souvenir.

Bill: Yes, it's the best gift that I can buy for my friend when I return to my country. OK, I'll take it.

Salesman: Shall I wrap it for you?

Bill: Yes, please. Can you wrap it in colored paper?

Salesman: Sure. Is it okay this way?

Bill: Great. Thanks. Can I use my credit card to pay the purchase?

Salesman: Yes, sir. We accept American Express, Visa and Matercard. Please go to the cashier.

Cashier: Here you go. Just sign the slip here, please. Have a nice day.

Bill: Thanks, you too.

比尔：我想给我朋友买点什么。你有什么好主意？

刘：当然有。你想买什么？

比尔：我想买有中国特色的东西。

刘：那你就买一些丝绸品，比如刺绣花边的手绢、桌布或者衬衫。

比尔：好主意！在哪能买到？

刘：我建议你去银街第一百货商店买。离这儿只有两街区远。

比尔：那儿东西贵吗？

刘：不贵。那儿价钱很合理。

比尔：太好了，谢谢你。

刘：不用谢。

(在百货商店)

售货员：你喜欢这丝巾吗？这是非常典型的中国纪念品。

比尔：是的，这是我回国以后能给朋友带的最好的礼物。好，我买了。

售货员：要给您包上吗？

比尔：好的，你能用彩纸包上吗？

售货员：当然可以。这样可以了吗？

比尔：太好了。谢谢。我能用信用卡付款吗？

售货员：可以先生，我们这可以用美国运通卡、维萨卡和万事达卡。请到收银台去付款。

出纳员：给您，请在这签名。祝您愉快！

比尔：谢谢，也祝你愉快。

Supplementary Reading

礼物

There Is No End to the Meaning of a Gift
By Douglas Todd

Is life an ordeal (痛苦的经历)? Or a gift?

Christmas—a worldwide festival marked by a torrent of shopping—is a worthwhile time to ask big questions about the meaning of gifts.

Canadians spend more than $22 billion on gifts from mid-November to late December. We often hear how the explosion of gift buying fuels the economy. Christmas accounts for one-quarter of Canadians' personal spending. The average Canadian, according to Ipsos Reid, spends about $640 on Christmas presents, including toys, cell phones, chocolates, babysitting, and bird feeders. You name it; it can be a gift.

But what is a gift?

The *Oxford Dictionary* says a gift is "a thing given willingly to another, without expectation of payment." Yet this strict definition does not come close to touching the far-reaching meaning of gifts. Most barely notice we are constantly making references to gifts: To the gift of musical talent, to charitable gifts, to the gift of listening, or the gift of life itself.

Yet it is Christmas that thrusts giving, literally, in our faces. We can't avoid children's eyes lighting up at a magical present from Santa. Giving and receiving Christmas presents can overwhelm people with feelings such as, "I don't deserve this," or "I am loved."

Christmas is also the time when carols (圣诞颂歌) tell of three sages (圣人) bringing gifts—of gold, frank-incense (乳香) and myrrh (没药树脂)—to a baby born 2,000 years ago to refugee (避难) parents in the Middle East. Spiritually, Christmas is the time for the planet's 2.2 billion Christians to celebrate the conviction that Jesus Christ is himself a gift, offered for the redemption (救赎) of all.

A gift is imbued (充满) with a unique glow. It's why we treasure a book or CD given to us more than if we buy them for ourselves. Unlike the impersonal (没有人情味的) exchange of money, gifts create relationships.

There is no end to the significance of giving. Consider how some thank their parents, or God, for the gift of their lives, and their talents. Cancer societies, Amnesty (大赦) International and food banks rely on charitable giving. Christians, Jews, Sikhs (锡克教徒), aboriginals (土著居民) and Hindus thank the Creator for the gift of life. Atheists (无神论者) are not immune to such sentiments, either. Secular (世俗的) people often express gratitude to others and the Earth.

Yet, as with every big subject, there is disagreement also about the meaning of gifts. Medical ethicists, who delve (探究) into abortion, euthanasia (安乐死) and genetic selection, often struggle with whether a human being is a gift, not to be altered. In addition, many think there is little room for giving in today's economy, where we are expected to toil (苦干) for financial security through merit. Gifts fuel the economy, and our lives. Yet giving somehow manages to penetrate our lives. Many think it should do so more. Many believe the spirit of giving should become a year-round ethic.

Reasons for Giving

You thought it was a straight-forward thing to give someone an iPod or a dining certificate? Christian Smith, a Notre Dame University professor who this year received a $5-million grant from the Templeton Foundation to study generosity, says people give for many different reasons, not all of them wonderful.

People give, says the sociologist, for strategic, impulsive, sentimental, habitual and ideological reasons, as well as out of guilt. Not to forget altruism (利他主义).

Even though research exploring the ins and outs of giving has become more serious in the past decade, psychologists already know many things about who gives and why. Studies show people who are religious respond to their faith's life-is-a-gift teachings by being more magnanimous (慷慨的), both to their own spiritual organization and beyond. In addition, research reveals generosity is good for you, with seniors who volunteer living longer. People who give more, says Smith, are "happier, healthier and doing better in life."

Gift-giving is not confined to Homo sapiens (智人), either. University of Washington bird expert John Marzluff has discovered that crows and other birds give trinkets (小玩意儿) or food. They do so to inspire loyalty, Marzluff says, and—like humans—for the enjoyment of it.

There is , however, at least one unfortunate thing researchers know about giving. People who have more money often give less, Smith says. Such research feeds the cynicism (愤世嫉俗) associated with Charles Dickens' classic story *A Christmas Carol*, supporting the Scrooge (吝啬鬼) theme that the rich are often more grasping and fearful.

Paul Zak, founder of Claremont Graduate University's Center for Neuroeconomics (神经经济学) Studies, has discovered gift-giving goes up with levels of oxytocin (后叶催产素)—the hormone (荷尔蒙) produced in the pituitary gland (脑下垂体) that is released during child-birth, and as people bond.

In one experiment, Zak's team gave an oxytocin nasal spray to half the subjects playing a game that required deciding whether to give money away. The oxytocin dose increased their generosity by 80%.

But let's not over-estimate the sometimes reductionist (还原论者) findings of neuroscience. It's not only people who are feeling good, via oxytocin or whatever, who give. Humans also feel good after they give. And so, often, does the receiver. Some call this the win-win benefit of paying it forward.

"There's something about learning how to get beyond one's self and helping other people that is good for the giver," says Smith, "And there is so much need in the world."

Gifts Create Relationships

Some philosophers, like the famous French deconstructionist Jacques Derrida, are sticklers for moral purity. Derrida has argued a gift is not a gift if there is any expectation of receiving anything in return—even a "Thank you."

Indeed, there is something to be said for the high value of an anonymous gift. But gifts are not always, or even often, about perfect altruism, or absolute sacrifice.

While there's no doubt gifts can be used to manipulate people, Derrida may not have fully grasped that gifts are mostly about cementing relationships. They may be given, as the *Oxford Dictionary* says, without expectation of payment. But sometimes gifts come with a sense of unspoken commitment, a covenant (承诺). And that's not bad. We're not autonomous (自主的) individuals. We're interdependent creatures. Sometimes we give, sometimes we take.

Unlike with the exchange of money, almost every gift creates a bond. That's why Washington state psychologist Bob Brizee wrote a book titled *The Gift of Listening*. And as another French thinker, playwright Jean Anouilh, said, "Love is, above all, the gift of oneself."

It doesn't take much to sully (玷污) a gift, though. Let's count the ways.

It's often not pretty sitting around a Christmas tree when gifts are distributed. The young can seem particularly greedy (贪婪的). Tearing open presents with abandon, children often act ungrateful. "This is not what I wanted!" Adults, too, can be spoiled by giving, whether it is one too many tony (时髦的) dresses or a flashy new four-by-four vehicle.

Gifts lose something when they're taken for granted. A gift needs to be exchanged in relative freedom.

When the mayor of Moscow brought in laws that forced all retailers to put up Christmas decorations to stimulate the economy, the ideal of lovingly exchanging gifts descended (沦为) into quasi-fascism (准法西斯主义).

Not that advertising-saturated (充斥着广告的) North Americans don't experience unnatural pressure to give. How many people have felt compelled by social expectation to toss money at the most costly or useless gifts? That not only leads to disappointment, it can contribute to unnecessary consumption, including of Earth's resources.

Americans throw away 25% more trash (废物) at Christmas than through the rest of the year, according to the Stanford Recycling Center.

When overzealous (过分热心的) givers descend into post-Christmas debt to hand over presents it's another sign giving has gone too far—as if the giver is desperate (极渴望的) for approval, or to make others dependent.

Self-restraint can be beneficial when it comes to giving.

Chapter 4
Etiquette of Practical Writings

文书礼仪

在本章中，你将了解到：
- 如何书写和回复邀请函
- 写信的格式和注意事项
- 如何写感谢信
- 发送电子邮件及传真的礼仪

Intensive Reading

4.1 Invitations

Invitations may be in form of cards, letters, telephone or Email. The level of formality of the invitation should accord with that of the occasion. It is common for westerners to send written invitations in formal occasions like luncheons, dinner parties, all other home parties, balls,

 weddings, etc. Generally speaking, formal invitations should be distributed in advance—three or more weeks before the occasion. This allows the invitee enough time to reply. In terms of a formal invitation, a printed card is usually used, which shows the event, date, time, location, R.S.V.P., the address, and phone number of the host/hostess. Other details are completed by hand. For in-home invitations, these are traditionally prepared in the name of the hostess only, in the case of married couples.

Most invitations contain "R.S.V.P." information. R.S.V.P. is the abbreviation for the French phrase, "Repondez, s'il vous plait," which means "Please reply." If so, please reply to the host/hostess in an appropriate time. Sometimes, the invitations list "Regrets only" which means "Please reply if you cannot come."

For invitations, it is good etiquette to write the full name of the guest, and not use initials. This applies to both the envelope and the invitation. When married guests are invited, there is no need to write the surname twice. For example, write "David and Louise Walker." It is acceptable to use Mr. And Mrs. Abbreviations or official ranks for invitations to truly formal events, such as weddings, anniversary parties, and bridal showers. When a family with young children is invited and if the inviter intends to invite all the children, "and family" or their first names will be written on the invitation. Otherw ise, the words "Adult Reception" will appear opposite the R.S.V.P. line on the invitation card.

Now, let us take a close look at wedding invitations, which comprise of several important elements.

(i) **Outer and inner envelope**. Most formal wedding invitations have an outer and an inner envelope. Some contemporary, less formal invitations have only the outer envelope. The outer envelope is where the recipient's address and full name are written (e.g., *Mr. and Mrs. John Smith*). Inviters only list the names of the couple or person they are inviting, not children or other guests. The return address is also printed on the flap.

An inner envelope reiterates whom it is for, with a more casual approach on inviting recipients to the ceremony (e.g., *Mr. and Mrs. Smith*). Inviters list the names of the invited guests on this envelope. If "and guest" is written, it indicates the invitee is welcome to bring a date. If the inviter wishes to invite children, their names would be listed in order of age from oldest to youngest. When there is no inner envelope, the names of all intended guests will be listed on the outer envelope or on the response card.

(ii) **Invitation.** Wedding invitations are usually written in the name of bride's parents. Here's a sample of invitation:

Mr. and Mrs. John Debrett

request the pleasure of

your company at the marriage

of their daughter

Caroline Jane

to

Mr. Richard Manners

at St. Paul's Church, Knightsbridge

on Saturday, 17th July 2011

at 3 o'clock

To respond to such an invitation, you may write a formal reply note, if you receive a wedding invitation that doesn't include a response card—which usually will only happen with very formal invitations. You need to use plain white or cream-colored notepaper and black ink. The wording is similar to the invite wording. Here's a sample of reply:

Mr. and Mrs. David Smith

thank Mr. and Mrs. John Debrett

for the kind invitation to the marriage

of their daughter

Caroline Jane

to

Mr. Richard Manners

at St. Paul's Church, Knightsbridge

on Saturday, 17th July

at 3 o'clock

and are delighted to accept/regret that they are unable to accept.

If you can accept the invitation, always repeat the date and time of the wedding to let your hosts know you understood their invitation. If you can't accept it, it is best to tell your hosts the reason why you decline it.

　　(iii) **Reception card.** There is always a reception following the wedding ceremony. A reception card is used to inform guests of the location and time of the wedding reception. In some cases this card is unnecessary. If both events are taking place all under one roof, "reception to follow" might be stated at the bottom of the invitation card. If the event has a reception in a location that requires guests to hop in their car right after the ceremony, then a reception card should be included.

　　(iv) **Response/Reply card.** Sometimes a special card is enclosed with the wedding invite. It is printed by the inviter for the convenience of the guests, usually with R.S.V.P. and response date deadline on it. Meanwhile, the inviter usually offers a reply envelope printed with his/her address and a postage stamp is affixed to it as well. Guests should fill in the card and post it back in good time.

　　The most common styles of R.S.V.P. wording are as follows:

The favor of a reply is requested

by July 25, 2011

M＿＿＿＿＿＿＿＿＿＿＿＿＿

＿＿＿＿Accepts with pleasure

＿＿＿＿Declines with regrets

　　The first line is meant for the guest to fill in Ms., Mr. or Mrs., and write their name(s). Then they simply check off whether or not they can come.

　　(v) **Map and travel instructions.** It is good etiquette to enclose map and travel instructions to help guests find the locations of ceremony and reception easily, especially for the guests who live far away.

4.2 Letters

　　Letters are equally important to make a good impression as meeting someone in person. Does it bother you when you receive a letter that is not well written, properly formatted, and presented? The answer probably is yes. So we'll explore how to write and format an English letter.

　　First list the date the letter is being sent, spelling out the entire date in either the American (April 1, 2004) or European (1 April 2004) styles. Then write the following information each on separate lines: Name of the recipient; street address, including suite number; city, state, zip code, and country (as appropriate). If it is a business letter, the recipient's title or position and company name are usually added before the address. As a sign of respect, especially for first-time letters to someone you have never met, it is best to address the person properly as Miss, Ms., Mrs. or Mr., followed by their first and last name. Follow this block of information with one or two line spaces.

All letters begin with "Dear" followed by the recipient's honorific and last name, followed by a colon, not a comma. For example, write "Dear Dr. Smith:" Again, "Dear Ms. Smith" is best for first time letters. As you become better acquainted with the person, you may just begin with "Dear" followed by the recipient's first name.

The most common layout style for the body text is to justify to the left margin and to place one or two extra line space to indicate new paragraphs. Whether you indent the first line (if you do, usually indent six spaces) or not is a matter of style and both are fine. The current style is to write letters in as conversational a manner as possible.

End letters with a cordial phrase you are comfortable using–Sincerely, Yours truly, or Best Regards—followed by a comma. Depending on space left at the bottom of the sheet, allow four to five lines spaces for a signature. When signing the letter, type your name using both your first and last name. In cases where a woman wishes to be addressed a specific way, be sure to add Mrs., Ms., or Miss in parenthesis before her name. If the letter is written by more than one person, include a signature line for each. A second signature line may be used to list the person's title or position, as applicable.

Your return address should be easy to find and read. It can be put down at either the top or the bottom of the letter as well as the top left corner or the flap of the envelope. For the fastest delivery service when addressing envelopes, you're advised to ensure that names are spelt correctly and that the correct form of the address is used. For instance, the address should be centered, insert one space between the city and state followed by a comma and two spaces between the state and zip code. Use only the two-letter state code. For foreign addresses, the country must be the last thing on the last line or in a separate field, whereas do not put anything after the zip code on domestic addresses.

Here's a sample of envelope:

Lockwood Middle School
307 Main Street
Lockwood, NJ 51686

A postage
stamp

Mrs. Betty Johnson
23 Main Street
Lockwood, NJ 68534

Here is a sample of letter:

Lockwood Middle School
307 Main Street
Lockwood, NJ 51686

December 10, 2008
Mrs. Betty Johnson
President
Lockwood Health Association
23 Main Street
Lockwood, NJ 68534

Dear Mrs. Johnson:

My name is Susan Harris and I am writing on behalf of the students at Lockwood Middle School.

A significant amount of the students at the school have been working on a project which relates to the unemployment problem within the youth demographic of Lockwood. You are invited to attend a presentation that will be held within the media room of the school where a variety of proposals that will demonstrate the ability of the community to develop employment opportunities for the youth within the community.

At the presentation, there will be several students receiving awards which will recognize them within the community from the Mayor. Refreshments will also be available at the presentation.

As one of the prominent figures in the community, we would be honored by your attendance. Our special presentation will be held at our school auditorium on January 16th. Please reply by Monday the 9th of January to confirm your attendance to the function.

We look forward to seeing you there.

Sincerely,

(Signature)
(Ms.) Susan Harris

4.3 Thank-you Note

Thank-you notes or thank-you letters are quite common and important in daily life. They are written for a dinner, a gift, a favor, or some other hospitality. It should be sent within a few days of the occasion. No matter what forms it takes, a card, a letter, or even an E-mail are fine. Whether a thank-you note is long or short doesn't matter, and the key point is sincerity. Don't hold back words to express your heart-felt appreciation and gratefulness. In addition, try to make the note sound as if you were talking to the recipient in person.

Here is an example of thank-you note for dinner:

Dear Kay and Bob,

We had so much fun with you last night! Thank you for that amazing dinner. The chicken was so fantastic that my kids are begging me to get the recipe—I can tell you that has never happened before! Everything was delicious, including of course that amazing dessert that looked so professional I still can't believe you MADE that.

We so appreciated your having us. It was great getting to know everyone better. We look forward to more fun in the future!

Thanks again.

Yours,

Lisa

Another sample of thank-you note for the gift:

Dear David,

Thank you so much for the lovely book! I have it out on our coffee table and everyone stops to browse through it. It's fascinating, and would you believe the cover design even matches our decor? It's perfect in every way.

Thank you again for thinking of me!

Much love,

Ann

4.4 Email and Fax Etiquette

4.4.1 Email Etiquette

Of all Internet activities, email is the most popular. According to the latest survey conducted by the University of California, Los Angeles (UCLA), almost 97% of all Internet users in the United States use email and nearly all of those who use the Internet at work use it to access business email (*The UCLA's World Internet Project: USA Digital Future Report*, 2011). This is the case with other western countries throughout the world.

It is important to pay attention to email etiquette because of the nature of reading emails. Reading text without sound, facial expression or tone of voice makes it harder to get the exact message across compared to face-to-face communication. That's why it is important to be as clear as possible to prevent miscommunication and misinterpretations.

In a formal situation, especially if you don't know the person, it is proper email etiquette to remain formal. This means complete your sentences, keep them short and sweet, write in paragraphs if you have to, spell out words the way they should be and punctuate. Keep slang and short form as limited as possible. Just as basic etiquette, courtesy and respect should always be employed. As with all letter writing etiquette, the email should start off addressing the recipient, e.g., *"To: Ashley Adams"* or *"Dear Ashley Adams."*

If you do not know "who" you are emailing to, you may send "To Whom It May Concern." When emailing to a generic email address, such as info@company.com, use *"To: Customer Service."*

You should also end off with, *"Yours Sincerely,"* of course depending on the formality of the message. The proper business email etiquette is to include a business phone number at where you sign off, also known as an "email signature."

Before sending your email, check to see if there are any glaring errors, such as misspellings and very poor grammar. Avoid typing in all capitals for it is ill-mannered. Remember to use the Subject field to concisely and accurately describe the contents. If you must forward an email to more than one person, put your email address in the "To:" field and all the others you are sending to in the "Bcc:" field to protect their email address from being published to those they do not know.

4.4.2 Fax Etiquette

For many companies, sending and receiving faxes are a daily occurrence. Faxing is so common that it is easy to slip into a casual communication. Following a few simple steps will help to keep your faxes looking professional. Proper fax etiquette will ensure your company maintains the professional reputation you've worked so hard to build.

When sending faxes, always remember to include a cover page, which is free of any unnecessary information. Your name and contact information, the number of pages (including the fax cover sheet), the intended recipient and any other relevant information should be listed on the cover sheet. The fax recipient may not be the only one who sees the document, so make sure to keep the fax cover sheet professional. After transmitting your fax, make a follow up call to the recipient. This does not require an in-depth discussion on what the fax contains. You are simply confirming the fax was received. It is appropriate in this conversation to let the person know they are free to call you with any follow up questions to the faxed materials at their convenience.

When receiving faxes, there are etiquette rules as well. If you receive a confidential fax, respect the privacy and do not share personal information with your coworkers that was intended solely for your viewing. If you receive a fax in error, let the sender know by giving them a call. Usually, it is requested that you destroy any faxes received in error.

Here is a sample of business fax cover sheet.

Company Name

Date _____

To _____   Fax _____

From _____   Fax _____

Total Pages _____

Cc _____

Re _____

□ Urgent □ For Review □ Please Comment □ Please Reply □ Please Recycle

If you have any problem, please call us at 86-21-55555555. Thank you!

◆ Vocabulary ◆

abbreviation /əˌbriːviˈeiʃən/ **n.** a shortened form of a word or phrase 缩写

shower /ˈʃauə/ **n.** a party of friends assembled to present gifts (usually of a specified kind) to a person 送礼会

invite /inˈvait/ **n.** a colloquial expression for invitation 请柬

contemporary /kənˈtempərəri/ **a.** belonging to the present time 当代的，现代的

flap /flæp/ **n.** any broad thin and limber covering attached at one edge (信封的) 封盖

reception /riˈsepʃən/ **n.** a formal party of people; as after a wedding 宴会

enclose /inˈkləuz/ **v.** enfold completely with or as if with a covering 随函附寄

postage /ˈpəustidʒ/ **n.** a token that postal fees have been paid 邮资

affix /əˈfiks/ **v.** attach to 粘贴

zip code /zip kəud/ a short sequence of letters and numbers at the end of your address, which helps the post office to sort the mail 邮政编码

honorific /ˌɔnəˈrifik/ **n.** an expression of respect 敬语

colon /ˈkəulən/ **n.** a punctuation mark (:) used after a word introducing a series or an example or an explanation (or after the salutation of a business letter)冒号

comma /ˈkɔmə/ *n.* a punctuation mark (,) used to indicate the separation of elements within the grammatical structure of a sentence 逗号

cordial /ˈkɔːdjəl/ *a.* showing warm and heartfelt friendliness 热诚的

parenthesis /pəˈrenθisis/ *n.* either of two punctuation marks (or) used to enclose textual material 圆括号

domestic /dəˈmestik/ *a.* of concern to or concerning the internal affairs of a nation 国内的

mis-interpretation/ˈmisinˌtəːpriˈteiʃən/ *n.* putting the wrong interpretation on 误解

punctuate /ˈpʌŋtʃueit/ *v.* insert punctuation marks into 加标点

slang /slæŋ/ *n.* informal language consisting of words and expressions that are not considered appropriate for formal occasions 俚语

glaring /ˈglɛəriŋ/ *a.* shining intensely 显眼的

forward /ˈfɔːwəd/ *v.* send or ship onward from an intermediate post or station in transit 发送, 转寄

Bcc *n.* Abbreviation for Blind Carbon Copy 密件抄送, 隐蔽副本

confidential /ˌkɔnfiˈdenʃəl/ *a.* (of information) given in confidence or in secret 机密的, 秘密的

◆ Exercises ◆

Ⅰ. Translation

Directions: *In this part there are 10 words or phrases in English. Please translate them into Chinese.*

> 1. R.S.V.P.   2. Regrets only.   3. reception card
> 4. response card   5. zip code   6. signature line
> 7. return address   8. Subject field   9. Bcc: field
> 10. fax cover sheet

Ⅱ. Blank filling

Directions: *In this part there is a short passage with several incomplete sentences. Please fill in all the blanks.*

　　Most formal wedding invitations have an outer and an inner envelope. The _____ envelope is where the recipient's address and _____ are written. An _____ envelope reiterates whom it is for, with a more casual approach. Inviters list the names of the invited guests on this envelope. If "_____" is written, it indicates the invitee is welcome to bring a date.

Wedding invitations are usually prepared in the name of _____'s parents. The invitation cards have fixed formats. If there is a reception following the wedding ceremony, a _____ is often used to inform guests of the location and time of the wedding reception. Sometimes a special _____ is enclosed with the wedding invite. It is printed by the inviter for the convenience of the guests, usually with R.S.V.P. and response date _____ on it. It is also a considerate act to enclose map instructions along with the invite.

III. Essay questions

Directions: *In this part there are two essay questions. Please write the corresponding answer for each question.*

1. Suppose you have been invited to dinner at your American friend, Sue's home at the weekend. Sue's family prepared a nice meal and you enjoyed it very much. Please write her a thank-you note.

2. What are the similarities and differences between writing an Email and a letter?

Situational Dialogues

Dialogue 1

(Inviting somebody to an engagement party)

Zhao: Hello?

Bob: Hi, Mr. Zhao.

Zhao: Yes.

Bob: This is Bob.

Zhao: Hi, Bob. How are you?

Bob: I'm fine. Hope I haven't called you too late tonight.

Zhao: Oh, no, no.

Bob: Oh, well. You must have been reading my mind because Alice and I are putting together a party that will start at 12:00 this Sunday.

Zhao: Great.

Bob: And, we'd like you to come, we haven't met up in a long time.

Zhao: Yeah, I think we should get together. What party?

Bob: We're having an engagement dinner party at the Guest Hotel this Sunday.

Zhao: All right, that sounds fun.

Bob: Yeah. Well, we're going to start to get together from about 11:00. We've just invited 3 other couples.

Zhao: OK, around 11:00.

Bob: Yeah, we'll be preparing and serving dinner at about 12:00. Please do get there before 12:00.

Zhao: Oh, no problem, will you prepare delicious Chinese dishes?

Bob: You bet.

Zhao: Okay, great! Can we bring anything? Wine?

Bob: Oh, maybe your dancing feet.

Zhao: Well, I'll be there on time.

Bob: OK. Well, thank you very much. Mr. Zhao, talk to you later.

Zhao: Bye-bye, my friend.

赵：喂。

鲍勃：喂，赵先生吗？

赵：是我。

鲍勃：我是鲍勃。

赵：喂，鲍勃你好吗？

鲍勃：很好，现在打电话给你太晚了吧？

赵：不晚不晚。

鲍勃：好的。你一定猜得出，因为我和爱丽丝准备本周日 12 点开个派对。

赵：太好了！

鲍勃：希望你能来，而且我们好久没见面了。

赵：是的，我们应该见面了，什么派对？

鲍勃：哦，我们办的是订婚宴会，这个星期天，在客人酒店。

赵：太好了，那就更有意义了。

鲍勃：我们聚会约 11:00 开始，我们只邀请了另外 3 对。

赵：好的，就 11:00。

鲍勃：我们准备 12:00 开饭，请在 12:00 之前到场。

赵：噢，没问题。准备好吃的中国菜了吗？

鲍勃：噢，当然要准备了。

赵：太棒了，我们带点什么？酒？

鲍勃：噢，带舞鞋吧。

赵：你真逗。我准时到。

鲍勃：好的。赵先生，十分感谢你。见面谈。

赵：再见。

Dialogue 2

(At Mr. Black's office)

Mr. Black: Miss Li, I'd like you to draw up a letter to a customer in Hong Kong.

Li: OK. Just a minute, please. *(Li takes a notebook and a pen in her hands.)* I'm ready now.

Mr. Black: Xiongwei Garments Corporation is our new customer. We want to establish business relations with them to expand our market in Hong Kong. We will enclose a copy of our brochure and a sample-cutting booklet together with this letter. Ask them if they are interested in our products. We will quote our best price as soon as we receive their enquiry. Is that clear?

Li: Yes, Mr. Black. By the way, since this letter is written to a new customer, I'd like to know where we have got their name and address.

Mr. Black: Yes, I almost forgot that. Thanks for reminding me. We got them from our Chamber of Commerce in Hong Kong.

Li: I see. I'll get it ready in half an hour.

(Half an hour later, Li presented the letter to Mr. Black.)

Mr. Black: *(After reading)* Not bad, Miss Li, it is quite clear and concise. But the whole letter doesn't seem to be as polite as it should be. Miss Li, you know we are now addressing a new customer and we hope that they will be willing to do business with us. Your "we attitude" in writing the letter may destroy the business opportunity, I'm afraid.

Li: Sorry.

Mr. Black: Besides, if you add more information about our business standing and business scope in a letter to a new customer, they'll be much more likely to establish business relations with us.

Li: I understand. It'll be better if we conclude the reference of our firm's financial position and integrity. Am I right?

Mr. Black: Definitely.

(Li is back again with her second draft.)

Mr. Black: *(After reading)* This one is much better. Miss Li, if business is possible between our two companies, you'll be the first to be rewarded.

Li: You're flattering me, Mr. Black. Please sign your name here.

Mr. Black: *(After signing)* Miss Li, if you receive such letters from our new customers, you'd better attend to it immediately. Otherwise it will be considered as impolite.

Li: I will, Mr. Black.

布莱克先生：李小姐，请你起草一份至香港一个客户的信件。

李：好的，请稍等。（李拿起了笔和记事本）好了，请讲。

布：雄伟服装公司是我们的新客户，我们想与他们建立业务关系以拓展我们在香港的市场。随函将附上我们的产品小册子和剪样各一份，告诉他们如果他们对我们的产品有兴趣，收到询盘后我们会立即报最低价。清楚了吗？

李：清楚了，布莱克先生。由于这封信是写给新客户的，我想顺便问一下我们从哪儿得知他们的地址和名称的。

布：哦，我差点忘了，谢谢你提醒了我。我们是从我国驻香港的商会那里得知的。

李：我明白了，我会在半小时内写完。

（半小时后，李把信交给了布莱克先生。）

布：（看过之后）李小姐，写得不错，相当清楚简洁，但整封信的语气不够礼貌。我们致函新客户，是希望与他们建立业务关系。但你写信时"以我为主"的态度，恐怕很可能会使我们丧失业务机会。

李：我很抱歉。

布：另外，在致函新客户时，介绍一下我方业务状况、经营范围，就会大大增加对方与我们建立业务关系的可能性。

李：明白了。如果信中再提供我们公司的资信情况证明的话就更好了，对吗？

布：完全正确。

（李拿着她的第二封草稿又回到了布莱克先生的办公室。）

布：（看过之后）李小姐，这次写得好多了。如果我们与香港公司之间的生意能成的话，你应该是第一位要受嘉奖的人。

李：布莱克先生，过奖了。请在这里签名。

布：（签完后）李小姐，如果你以后收到类似的信件，应迅速完整地答复，否则是不礼貌的。

李：我会的，布莱克先生。

Supplementary Reading

汉字的来源与演变

The Peril of Online Invitations: Who's Invited?

By KJ Dell'Antonia

I'm all for online birthday invitations. What could be easier? One click to respond, a few more and it's on the calendar. Easy-peasy (轻而易举地), especially for a parent with a nice full box in the basement of suitable gifts for any birthday child. I have birthdays covered.

Except when I can't tell which of my children is invited.

I know, I know. This, in the grand scheme of problems, or even social perils (危险，问题), is small potatoes. We'll struggle through somehow. But please, kind fellow parents who are planning to host one or more of my children [or any children from a family with close-in-age siblings(兄弟，姐妹)]: Could you possibly be a little more specific?

My three youngest children are 5, 6 and 7 (next week, 6, 6 and 7). Two are in the same class at school, and they all share friends and play dates regularly. So that online birthday party invitation addressed to my e-mail address tells me nothing about which child is expected. And asking—while the sensible, obvious solution—nearly always provokes "Oh, both (or all) of them! Of course!"

But I am on to you, my fellow parents: you lie. You are trying to be polite, I am trying to be polite. Can't we find a way to be polite and honest at the same time?

I'd have thought I was the only person with this problem, if one of you hadn't written to me about it earlier this week. In her case, she keeps scrupulously (细致缜密地)bringing only one of her two preschool-age sons to a party (the one closest in age to the celebrated child) and finding a bouncy (充满活力的) house full of happy siblings, and mystified hosts: Why didn't you bring along number two?

Because he wasn't asked, of course. Or maybe he was. Who knows? A month ago, I erred in the other direction: an online invitation for a joint party for two siblings, a girl my oldest daughter's age, a boy my youngest son's age. My younger daughter had other plans (a handwritten and mailed birthday invitation for her only), and the way seemed clear—except that once we got there, it was obvious (those cursed goody bags) that although both of my children were welcome, only one had been on the guest list.

Earlier this week, I got a lovely e-mailed invitation from one of my most gracious and socially adept (擅长的)friends. It was addressed, at the top, to all of the invited children, and I could have hugged her. One simple line of text made my life much easier, and it's a gesture I'll be sure to repeat.

Have you pondered (思索)over an invitation, trying to decide which child was the intended recipient? Or have you had a sibling appear, uninvited, at a child's party? (Maybe now you know why.) And have you asked, or been asked, if a sibling was included—and maybe not given, or received, a straight answer? Just for fun, dish here. And can we all promise to spell it out when the next child's birthday rolls around (周而复始)?

Chapter 5

Etiquette of Behavior in Public Places

公共场所行为礼仪

在本章中，你将了解到：

- 西方人的个人空间距离
- 如何在公共场合使用手机
- 观看演出时应注意些什么
- 乘车礼仪
- 小费礼仪

Intensive Reading

5.1 Personal Space

Westerners attach much importance to personal space. They believe all people have a comfort zone, an invisible zone of psychological comfort that people carry with them. It's the region surrounding each person, or the area which a person considers their territory. It's the space that someone keeps between them and the person standing in front of them. They call it their personal space.

In 1966, Edward T. Hall, an anthropologist, introduced the term *proxemics*. What is proxemics? It is the study of the cultural, behavioral, and sociological aspects of spatial distances between individuals; it is the study of set measurable distances between people as they interact; and it has to do with the study of our use of space and how various differences in that use can make us feel more relaxed or anxious.

Different cultures maintain different standards of personal space. Mr. Hall has broken down the distances of personal territory (for Americans) into 4 areas:

- 0 to18 inches: Intimate distance
- 18 inches to 4 feet: Personal distance for interactions among good friends or family members
- 4 feet to 12 feet: Social distance for interactions among acquaintances
- 12 feet to 25 feet or more: Public distance used for public speaking

Comfortable personal distances also depend on the social situation, gender, and individual preference.

Personal space in the West shows westerners' general aversion to touching others and being touched, especially in public places. The "keep to the right" rule (see below) is one means of reducing the likelihood that strangers will have physical contact with each other. In cases where they bump into another person or otherwise touch the other person indeliberately, they will quickly draw away and apologize, making clear that the touch was accidental. They will say "Excuse me" or "Sorry." The behavior of queuing is another means of avoiding touching, which is much less likely to happen in a line than in a crowd jostling to get service.

Keep to the Right: *When westerners are walking in two opposite directions in groups—on* *sidewalks, in hallways, or on stairways—wherever groups of people are walking in two opposite directions, they usually stay on the right side. This enables them to pass each other without physical contact and to progress as quickly as possible.*

5.2 The Use of Cell Phones in Public

There is no doubt that cell phones have a permanent and essential role in modern society. When cell phones interrupt important proceedings and are used in the wrong place at the wrong time, it is unacceptable and makes people grind their teeth in despair at the users' rudeness and blatant lack of care and consideration for the people around them.

The following are some of the places and events where cell phones should be switched off or the ring tone silenced. If it is vitally important to be reached in such places, then the call should be kept brief and the voice low:

- On public transport in proximity to other commuters
- In hospitals, restaurants, and shopping centers
- At checkouts, cinemas, and theaters
- Train stations, bus stops, and airports
- Doctors' surgeries, churches, and conventions
- Waiting rooms, libraries, and lecture rooms
- At christenings, weddings, and funerals

It's not the use of cell phones that is the problem; it's the loud and annoying ring tone. It's the shouting into the cell phone; it's the airing of one's private life on the cell phone in the presence of strangers.

It is bad cell phone etiquette to make a call whilst in the company of another person. In fact, it is downright rude. If you absolutely must make that call, apologize first, then make or accept the call. Of course, you should keep it very brief. Sending text messages in company is even worse. Once again, if unavoidable, excuse yourself first and then be very brief. Share the message with those present as a courtesy to let them know that they are not the subject of the message.

It is unforgivable to talk on a mobile phone while "dealing" with another person such as a checkout in a shop or bank-teller or greeting someone or bidding someone farewell.

Last, let us talk about camera cell phones. These are so useful and handy. You should be aware of privacy laws and the rights of others if used inappropriately in the wrong places.

Practicing good cell phone etiquette will not improve your popularity but it will certainly not make you unpopular. Importantly, you will not be contributing to cell phone rage.

5.3 At Concerts

Etiquette for different concerts varies from one sort of situation to another. For example, the audience at a rock concert might make much more noise than those at opera or western classical music. And the dress codes are also quite different. In this section, we'll talk about the etiquette of attending classical concerts or opera.

5.3.1 Before the Performance

Before you arrive at the theater, come dressed for the occasion. Classical performances are very special occasions. See all of those musicians on the stage? They are the best at their profession. They've been schooled at some of the finest institutions in the world. They're all wearing tuxedos or formal dress. While it is not necessary for attendants to dress in "black tie formal," at least make the effort to dress in your Sunday best. Jeans, T-shirts, and shorts are not appropriate attire for a night at the symphony or opera (see Chapter 7 for details).

Arrive at the theater on time. Fifteen minutes earlier will be appropriate, which allows you enough time to complete your "other" business before the start of the show. This includes cell phone calls (cell phones should be turned off completely anyway) and trips to the bathroom or concession stand. It's extremely annoying to have a door to the atrium opened during performances. As a courtesy to the performers, the doors should remain shut until between movements. Food and drink (excluding water) are not allowed in the theater as well.

Upon entering the theatre, you should certainly take off your hat. Hats are not tolerated as they block the view of the stage. If your ticket has a row and seat number, be sure to sit in the seat you are given. If it is a general admission ticket, have respect to the arrangement of the usher. When waiting for a concert to begin, you may talk freely until the end of the applause greeting the entrance of the conductor.

5.3.2 During the Performance

The convention of silence during performances developed long ago. Keep quiet and do not talk. It's not only distracting to those around you, but also annoys the performers. Unavoidable noises such as coughs or sneezes should be delayed until a loud passage or confined until between movements if possible. Coughs or sneezes should be muffled with a handkerchief or most effectively, placed at the inner elbow joint with the entire arm then pressed over the mouth. As common courtesy, do not photograph or videotape without permission.

Remember, classical concerts are not rock concerts. In other kinds of music, the audience claps whenever there's an ending—if the music stops, people applaud. But in classical music, one piece may have several parts, each with its own ending. You should save your applause for the very end of the very last ending, and only at that time be enthusiastic about it. If you are not familiar with the music, take your cue from the other attendees.

5.3.3 After the Performance

Stay in your seat for the curtain call. A curtain call occurs at the end of a performance when individuals return to the stage to be recognized by the audience for their performance. Do applaud enthusiastically to show your appreciation. Stand and applaud if you really like it. Performers are thrilled when they receive such a special honor called *standing ovations*. A standing ovation is a form of applause where members of a seated audience stand up while applauding after

Standing Ovation

extraordinary performances of particularly high acclaim. Often it is used at the departure of a performer, where the audience members will continue the ovation until the ovated person leaves.

In western opera, shouting is generally acceptable only during applause; almost always the Italian word *bravo*, which means "well done," is used even at the symphony. Shouting the French word *encore*, which means "again," at the end of a concert is understood as request for more. While particularly enthusiastic audiences may applaud with whistling in some cultures (e.g., Britain), this can—on the contrary—be an expression of disapproval in others (e.g., Italy). It is equivalent to booing.

5.4 Riding Public Transportation and Cars

5.4.1 Buses/Trains/Subways

Basic courtesies are easily forgotten on public transportation, particularly if delays are lengthy and space is tight. The whole public transportation experience—may it be by bus, train, or subway—is immeasurably improved by good manners.

Wait in the queue at the station and don't push others. Before boarding the bus, train, etc., wait for other passengers to exit first, never jostle past people who are trying to get off.

Always give up your seat to someone who is elderly, disabled or obviously pregnant. Mothers with small children in tow should also be given priority.

Some public transportation is very quiet, packed with commuters reading newspapers or working on their laptops, so be aware that loud mobile phone conversations are very disturbing. You'd better text rather than be on a call. If you are going to listen to the music on your MP3 player, ensure that you have sound-proof headphones and turn down the volume.

If you are riding alone, keep to yourself. Staring blankly at objects is normal on public transportation, but do not stare at other people. If you are riding with friends, keep conversation personal and quiet. Avoid private life stories, and speak in a low tone. And most of all, avoid using offensive language, arguing, or fighting on the train; it is simply rude.

Also be aware that eating greasy, smelly food (such as burgers or oily onions) may disgust your fellow passengers, and is a major cause of litter.

There are usually joint seats on public transportation. At peak times of the day, public transportation is naturally packed. Don't take up an additional seat with your excess baggage. If you are sitting on an aisle seat and the person on the window seat has left, you must automatically take their window seat. Not only will you have a better view, but you are politely allowing people who are standing in the aisle to have a seat.

Always stand back from the doors. If the public transportation is crowded and you happen to stand by a door, when it pulls into the station, and you are not getting off, get off anyway and allow people to exit the transport, then rush back in.

5.4.2 Taxis

Taking a ride in a taxi (AmE. *cab*) is a quick and convenient way to get wherever you want. When you see a taxi with its light on, i.e., available for hire, simply lift your arm and lean out from the pavement slightly to get the taxi driver's attention. Refrain from shouting "Taxi," waving frantically, or giving a piercing whistle.

Enter the taxi and give the driver your destination address. But in some countries like the UK, you are suggested to tell the driver your destination before getting in. Men should allow women to get in first. Ideally, men open the door for women and women stay on that side of the seat. Then men go around to the other side and get in.

If you find yourself in a situation where you need your taxi driver to take you to a variety of places—perhaps from the airport to your hotel and onto a convention center—ask about an hourly rate. Not only may an hourly rate be cheaper, but it will also free you of the stress that comes from keeping the meter running. If you need the taxi to wait for you while you run into your hotel and change, an hourly rate will allow you to be less in a hurry and less likely to forget something as you run out the door.

Whenever you get inside a taxi, it's a good idea to write down relative information: The driver's name, the taxi's number, the time, date, and destination of your route. This not only helps you in the instance you want to complain about service, but it also helps you get items returned if you happen to forget something in the backseat.

At your destination pay the driver and exit at the curbside so you don't risk injury from oncoming traffic. In British style, get out and pay the driver through the front window. And do not forget to tip. Usually, it's best to tip a taxi driver what you would tip a waiter or a waitress, which is 15% to 20% of the total fare. If the taxi driver is exceptionally good—if he takes a short cut to get you to an urgent meeting, for example—then tip him more. If he is rude or made a point of going ridiculously slow when there is no traffic, then don't feel too guilty when you tip him less.

5.4.3 Cars

Cars are so much a part of our everyday lives that we take them for granted and usually forget that driving manners cannot be separated from safety. Here are general tips that should be helpful for both drivers and passengers.

If it's your car and you are in the driver's seat, you are the boss. It's up to you to make sure your car is in good condition and is sufficiently fueled. You have every right to ask your passengers to buckle their seat belts and to insist that very young children have child safety seats. Pets, too, should be contained properly when you are driving. It is also up to the driver to suggest where people sit. The seat of honor is the front passenger seat. It is polite to defer to older persons and give them that seat. In a business situation, the client or the highest-ranking person gets that seat. If a couple has a single person in the car, it is best to offer the front seat to that person rather than to isolate him or her in the back. However, accommodating a passenger with long legs may have to take precedence over the above considerations.

If you're a passenger in someone else's car, your behavior must be polite and gracious at all times, just as it would be if you were visiting their home. The driver is in control of the car and that extends to the controls of the stereo, temperature, etc., Don't adjust anything or fiddle with the controls without asking first. If there are lots of you in the car, be aware of people's personal space. Try to keep to your own seat and give other people as much room as possible.

Engage in conversation but spare a thought for the driver, who has to concentrate on what he or she is doing, and stay quiet during tricky movements and challenging situations. It is irritating and rude to your driver and fellow passengers to engage in lengthy phone conversations. Answer any urgent calls but try to arrange to call the person back later.

It is the height of rudeness to smoke in someone else's car without their permission. Never smoke in a car when children are present. If you have anything to eat or drink, be careful not to spill a drop, or leave crumbs. Don't eat smelly foods in confined spaces and take all your rubbish with you before getting out of the car.

5.5 Tipping

Tipping etiquette can be quite a dilemma, especially when travelling overseas. Being prepared will prevent it from becoming an embarrassing situation. Travel tipping creates one of the biggest problems facing the traveler in countries where tipping is the norm and expected. Who to tip? How much to tip? How little to tip without appearing stingy?

In countries where tipping is the custom, tipping is commonplace in taxis, in restaurants and bars, in hotels, and in hair and beauty salons.

There are two types of tipping. One is proffered according to the proportion of the bill. Tip 10% of the commodity charge for ordinary service (15% in the USA and Canada), and up to 15% for superior service (20% in the USA and Canada). Tipping in restaurants is usually "discretionary," but it is more discretionary in some places than others. Check your bill. "Service not included" means just that, and it is usual to offer 10% to 20%. If you are paying by card, you will often be able to add the tip before entering your PIN number. This is fine, but leaving a cash tip is more likely to reach the waiting staff themselves.

The other type of tipping is proffered according to the convention. In smarter hotels, tipping will be expected. Give a small gratuity (i.e., one or two dollars/pounds) to bellboys or porters per piece of luggage if they take your bags to your room. Doormen should be tipped upon checking out if they have helped with taxis or luggage. If a parking valet parks your car for you, two dollars/pounds are expected. A banknote (i.e., at least two dollars/pounds) may be left in your room for housekeeping. Check whether a service charge is included in your room service bill. If not, add 10% to 20% at the end of your stay and ask that it be given to the appropriate staff members.

Generally speaking, pay a dollar/pound or two for minimal service provided and 10 to 15 dollars/pounds for excellent service that will prevent you from a tricky situation.

In many cases, even when the tip is added to the bill as a service charge, a further tip is expected. The service industry is notorious for this practice. In the USA, restaurant tipping etiquette requires that a service provider be paid 15% to 20% of the bill rendered. Some European countries would be happy with a tip of 10% to 15%. In Australia and New Zealand there is no such thing as tipping etiquette. Employees are paid a decent wage so tipping is generally not expected.

◆ Vocabulary ◆

psychological /ˌsaikəˈlɔdʒikəl/ *a.* mental or emotional as opposed to physical in nature 心理的

territory /ˈteritəri/ *n.* a region marked off for administrative or other purposes 领域，地盘

proxemics /prɔkˈsiːmiks/ *n.* the study of spatial distances between individuals in different cultures and situations 空间关系学

sociological /ˌsəuʃiəˈlɔdʒikəl/ *a.* of or relating to or determined by sociology 社会学的

spatial /ˈspeiʃəl/ *a.* pertaining to or involving or having the nature of space 空间的

intimate /ˈintimit/ *a.* marked by close acquaintance, association, or familiarity 亲密的

aversion /əˈvəːʒən/ *n.* a feeling of intense dislike 厌恶

queue /kjuː/ *v.* form a queue, form a line, stand in line 排队 *n.* a line of people or vehicles waiting for something 队列

jostle /ˈdʒɔsəl/ *v.* make one's way by jostling, pushing, or shoving 挤, 推

proceeding /prəˈsiːdiŋ/ *n.* an event or a series of things that happen 进程

grind /graind/ *v.* press or grind with a crunching noise 磨碎

blatant /ˈbleitnt/ *a.* without any attempt at concealment; completely obvious 公然的

mute /mju:t/ *v.* deaden (a sound or noise), especially by wrapping 消除，减轻(声音)

proximity /prɔk'simiti/ *n.* the property of being close together 接近

commuter /kə'mju:tə/ *n.* someone who travels regularly from home in a suburb to work in a city (远距离)上下班往返的人

surgery /'sə:dʒəri/ *n.* a room where a doctor or dentist can be consulted 外科诊所

christening /'krisniŋ/ *n.* giving a Christian name at baptism 洗礼仪式

farewell /'fɛə'wel/ *n.* the act of departing politely 告别

inappropriately /ˌinə'prəupriətli/ *ad.* in an inappropriate manner 不合适地

tuxedo /tʌk'si:dəu/ *n.* semiformal evening dress for men 无尾晚礼服

attire /ə'taiə/ *n.* clothing of a distinctive style or for a particular occasion 服装

symphony /'simfəni/ *n.* long and complex sonata for symphony orchestra 交响乐

concession /kən'seʃən/ *n.* a refreshment stand at a recreational center (大型建筑物里的)摊位

atrium /'eitriəm/ *n.* the central area in a building 中庭

movement /'mu:vmənt/ *n.* a major self-contained part of a symphony or sonata 乐章

applause /ə'plɔ:z/ *n.* a demonstration of approval by clapping the hands together 鼓掌

conductor /kən'dʌktə/ *n.* the person who leads a musical group 指挥

distract /dis'trækt/ *v.* draw someone's attention away from something 使……分心

muffle /'mʌfəl/ *v.* deaden (a sound or noise), especially by wrapping 捂住

enthusiastic /in,θju:zi'æstik/ *a.* having or showing great excitement and interest 热烈的

ovation /əu'veiʃən/ *n.* enthusiastic recognition (especially one accompanied by loud applause) 热烈欢迎

acclaim /ə'kleim/ *n.* clap one's hands or shout after performances to indicate approval 喝彩

boo /bu:/ *v.* show displeasure, as after a performance or speech 发出嘘声

tow /təu/ *n.* the act of hauling something (as a vehicle) by means of a hitch or rope 拖，拉

laptop /'læp,tɔp/ *n.* portable computer small enough to use in your lap 手提电脑

greasy /'gri:si/ *a.* containing an unusual amount of grease or oil 油腻的

refrain /ri'frein/ *v.* not do something 克制

frantically /'fræntikəli/ *ad.* in an uncontrolled manner 疯狂地

piercing /'piəsiŋ/ *a.* high-pitched and sharp 尖锐的，刺耳的

curbside /'kə:bsaid/ *n.* the side of a sidewalk that is bordered by a curb 靠近路缘的人行道部分

ridiculously /ri'dikjuləsli/ *ad.* so as to arouse or deserve laughter 荒谬地

accommodate /ə'kɔmədeit/ *v.* have room for; hold without crowding 提供(膳宿、座位等)

gracious /'greiʃəs/ *a.* exhibiting courtesy and politeness 有礼貌的

stereo /'stiəriəu/ *n.* reproducer in which two microphones feed two or more loudspeakers to give a three-dimensional effect to the sound 立体声

fiddle /'fidl/ *v.* manipulate manually or in one's mind or imagination 用手胡乱拨弄

irritating /'iri,teitiŋ/ *a.* causing irritation or annoyance 恼人的

dilemma /di'lemə/ *n.* state of uncertainty or perplexity especially as requiring a choice between

equally unfavorable options 困境

stingy /ˈstindʒi/ *a.* not generous 吝啬的

commonplace /ˈkɔmənpleis/ *a.* completely ordinary and unremarkable 普通的

proffer /ˈprɔfə/ *v.* present for acceptance or rejection 提供

commodity /kəˈmɔditi/ *n.* articles of commerce 商品

discretionary /diˈskreʃəˌnəri/ *a.* having or using the ability to act or decide according to your own discretion or judgment 随意的

gratuity /ɡrəˈtuːiti/ *n.* a relatively small amount of money given for services rendered (as by a waiter) 小费

bellboy /ˈbelˌbɔi/ *n.* someone employed as an errand boy and luggage carrier around hotels 行李生

porter /ˈpɔːtə/ *n.* a person employed to carry luggage and supplies 搬运工

doorman /ˈdɔːmən/ *n.* someone who guards an entrance 门卫

valet /ˈvælit/ *n.* a service employee who parks cars for guests 泊车员

banknote /ˈbæŋknəut/ *n.* a piece of paper money (especially one issued by a central bank) 纸币

notorious /nəuˈtɔːriəs/ *a.* having an exceedingly bad reputation 声名狼藉的

◆ Exercises ◆

Ⅰ. Translation

Directions: *In this part there are 10 words or phrases in English. Please translate them into Chinese.*

1. personal space   2. keep to the right   3. text message

4. porter   5. waiting staff   6. usher

7. curtain call   8. standing ovation   9. public transportation

10. window seat

Ⅱ. Blank filling

Directions: *In this part there are two short passages with several incomplete sentences. Please fill in all the blanks.*

Passage 1

Different cultures maintain different standards of personal space. Edward T. Hall, an anthropologist, has broken down the distances of personal territory (for US Americans) into 4 areas: _____ distance，personal distance for interactions among good friends or family members, _____ distance for interactions among acquaintances, and public distance used for public speaking.

_____ in the West shows westerners' general aversion to touching others and being touched especially in public places. The "_____" rule is one means of reducing the likelihood that strangers will have physical contact with each other. In cases where they bump into another person or otherwise touch the other person inadvertently, they will quickly draw away and _____, making clear that the touch was accidental. They will say "_____" or "Sorry." The behavior of _____ is another means of avoiding touching, which is much less likely to happen in a line than in a crowd jostling to get service.

Passage 2

In countries where tipping is the custom, tipping is commonplace in taxies, in _____ and bars, in hotels, and in hair and beauty salons. Usually you need to tip a taxi driver what you would tip a waiter or a waitress, which means _____ percent of the overall _____ when you travel in the United States. In more upscale hotels, give a small gratuity about _____ dollars to bellboys or porters per piece of _____ if they take your bags to your room. If a parking valet parks your car for you, _____ dollars are expected. And at least _____ dollars may be left in your room for housekeeping.

III. Essay questions

Directions: *In this part there are two essay questions. Please write the corresponding answer for each question.*

1. Suppose when you travel in Europe, you have got an opera ticket with a reserved seat. You will go to the theater to enjoy the performance this evening. What are the key points you should take care of before, during, and after the performance?

2. You are invited to a dinner by your British friend. The host and hostess are so considerate that they come in their car to fetch you to their house. Which seat should you take if one of them is the driver? Along the journey, your cell phone rings. What would you do then?

Situational Dialogues

Dialogue 1

(Talking about Peking Opera)

Lisa: Please do me a favor. Accompany Mr. Smith to the Youth Theater tomorrow night.

Wang: OK. What's on then?

Lisa: Peking Opera *Merry New Year*.

Wang: I've once seen it already and I just plan to see it again.

Lisa: I know you are an opera fan. You see, this Mr. Smith is an expert of Peking Opera.

Wang: Really?

Lisa: Yes. But he wants to know more about other Chinese operas.

Wang: This opera is performed by the China Beijing Opera Troupe, one of the best in China. Their costumes are very fascinating and there are many make-ups of different colors.

Lisa: Then Mr. Smith will enjoy it.

丽莎：请帮我一个忙，明晚陪史密斯先生到青年剧院去看戏。

王：好的，什么戏？

丽莎：京剧《贺新年》。

王：我看过的，但正想再看一遍呢。

丽莎：我知道你是个戏迷，但是这位史密斯先生也是个京剧专家哟。

王：真的？

丽莎：是啊。不过他想更多地了解一下其他的中国戏剧。

王：这部剧是由中国最好的京剧团之一——中国京剧院表演的。他们的表演服装特别有意思，还有许多不同颜色的脸谱。

丽莎：那么史密斯先生一定会喜欢的。

Dialogue 2

(Taking a taxi)

Taxi Driver: Good morning, where to?

Yang: Stanford University. How long will it take? I'm in a great hurry.

Driver: Usually just 10 minutes, but it all depends on the traffic.

Yang: I hope there is no traffic jam.

Driver: The rush hour is just over. It shouldn't be too bad.

Yang: Could you drop me off at the corner?

Driver: Sure. Here you are.

Yang: How much do I owe you?

Driver: 75 dollars.

Yang: Here is 80 dollars. Keep the change please.

Driver: Thanks. Have a nice day.

出租车司机：你好，去哪儿？

杨：去斯坦福大学。需要多长时间？我很急。

司机：一般来说，只有 10 分钟，但得看交通状况。

杨：希望没有交通堵塞。

司机：高峰期刚过，应该不会太糟。

杨：你能让我在那个拐角下车吗？

司机：可以，我们到了。

杨：我应该给你多少钱？

司机：75 美元。

杨：这是 80 美元，不用找了。

司机：谢谢，祝您愉快。

Dialogue 3

(In the hall of subway station)

Li: Do they accept bills here?

Joan: We need a token.

Li: A token? What do you mean?

Joan: A token is a subway pass. You pay 8.5 dollars and get a coin-like yellow metal piece. You insert it into the slot of the check in path. The fence will be open for you to the platform. Look, we'll get two tokens.

(在地铁大厅里)

李：他们这里收纸币吗？

琼：我们得买一个代币。

李：代币？代币是什么？

琼：代币是地铁通行币。你花 8.5 美元买一个像硬币一样的黄色金属圆片。在地铁检票口处把圆片放到投币孔里，检票口的门档就开了，你就可以进站台上车了。看，我们要买两个代币。

Dialogue 4

(At a bus station)

Zhao: How often does this bus run at this time of day?

Sarah: It runs every 15 minutes.

Zhao: Oh, here it is coming.

Sarah: Just drop your money into the box.

Zhao: Gosh, I have no change with me.

Sarah: If I were you, I would buy a lot of tokens at one time. You know, in this city the same tokens can be used on either the bus or the subway.

Zhao: This is really a good way.

赵：现在这个时候隔多久有一班车呀？

莎拉：每 15 分钟有一班车。

赵：哦，车来了。

莎拉：把钱投到盒子里就可以了。

赵：完了，我没有带零钱。

莎拉：如果我是你，我会买很多代币。你知道在这个城市，一样的代币可以在任何一辆公交车或地铁上使用。

赵：这真是个好办法。

 Supplementary Reading

中国戏曲

Tipping Doesn't Reward Good Behavior

By Ryan Sager

An urban legend about the origin of tips has it that the term comes from signs hung on boxes put out at British pubs in the 18th century to solicit (请求) gratuities: To Ensure Promptness. The tale is apocryphal (不足凭信的), but it encapsulates (概括) our accepted understanding of what a tip is and why we do (or don't) give one.

With more than $40 billion spent on tips in the food-service industry alone every year and that's just in the USA we'd like to think we know why we're giving all this money away. As it is so often, however, our grasp on what motivates our behavior is tenuous (含糊的).

Tipping did, in fact, migrate here from Europe after the Civil War. And it caused some controversy. Americans have long been suspicious of tipping as undemocratic. And yet in fields from food service to hair cutting to taxi driving, tipping has become an ingrained (根深蒂固的) part of our culture.

So why do we do it? It turns out that our most common understanding that tipping is meant to reward and encourage good service doesn't hold much water.

If your tip is meant to improve your service the next time around, practically no one should tip while taking a cab or dining out of town. But studies show that we do tip in these situations and, in the case of eating out, at essentially the same rate as when we dine in a restaurant regularly.

What's more, our tips don't actually vary that much with the level of service we've received. While people claim in surveys that they tip almost exclusively based on the level of service, field studies in actual restaurants, such as those conducted by Michael Lynn of Cornell University, find that better service is only partially correlated with bigger tips. A step up on a 1 to 5 rating scale of customer satisfaction translates into just a small increase (say, from 15% to 16% or 17% of the check).

What does make us tip better? How about breasts? A 2009 study published in the *Archives of Sexual Behavior* found that larger self-reported breast size among waitresses correlated with bigger tips. Similarly, a 2010 study in the *International Journal of Hospitality Management* found that waitresses' use of makeup significantly increased their tips. Female servers can also increase their tips by drawing a smiley (微笑的) face on the back of customers' checks (male servers, it turns out, can't achieve the same with this tactic [手段]).

In fairness to men: Women do tip male servers better than they tip female servers though waiters' attractiveness doesn't seem to enter into the equation (等式).

Studies also have found that complimenting (赞美) a diner's choice of dishes can boost tips (compliments also go a long way in boosting tips at hair salons, too). Also effective: A touch on the customer's arm, stooping (俯身) down to table level, a flower in the hair, introducing oneself by name and giving diners extra candy at the end of a meal.

The key to tipping, then, has less to do with reward or punishment for quality of service. It's about rewarding or punishing those who engage our interest or empathy. A little more flirting (调情的) goes a lot further than a little faster refill on your coffee.

Chapter 6
Dining Etiquette

餐饮礼仪

在本章中，你将了解到：
- 西餐的餐具摆放
- 西餐的菜式
- 如何使用餐巾
- 餐桌礼仪
- 座次安排
- 西方人的付账习俗

Intensive Reading

6.1 The Table Setting

Table setting is of great importance for western-style meals, especially for formal occasions. Utensils are arranged in the order and the way a person will use them. Usually in Western culture, t hat means that the forks, bread plate, spreader, and napkin are to the left. Knives, spoons, drinkware, cup, and saucers are to the right. Note that the left to right order is reversed in a minority of countries. Remembering the rule of "liquids on your right" and "solids on your left" will help you quickly be familiar with the place setting.

At an informal setting, fewer utensils are used and serving dishes are placed on the table. Sometimes the cup and saucer are placed on the right side of the spoon, which is about four inches from the edge of the table.

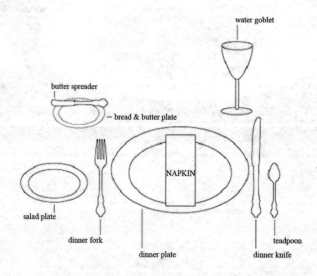

Informal Table Setting

At a formal setting, utensils are placed about one inch from the edge of the table, each one lining up at the base with the one next to it. Utensils on the outermost position are used first (e.g., a salad fork and a soup spoon, then the dinner fork and the dinner knife). The blade of the knife, must face toward the plate, away from other diners. The glasses are positioned about an inch from the knives, also in the order of use: White wine, red wine, dessert wine, and water glass.

Dishes from the most formal dinners are served from the kitchen. When the meal is served and in addition to the place plate at each setting, there is the roll, the napkin, and the following cutlery: Forks on the left and knives (and spoons where applicable) on the right. Serving dishes and utensils are not placed on the table for a formal dinner. At a less formal dinner, not served from the kitchen, the dessert fork and spoon can be set above the plate. The fork points to the right to match the other forks, and the spoon points to the left. The utensils at a formal dinner must be sterling silver. In Europe, if many courses are to be served, the table is only laid for soup, fish, and meat. The desert spoon and fork are then placed on the table as required.

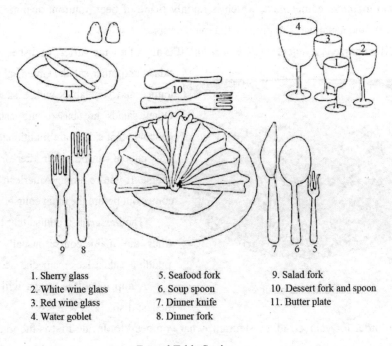

1. Sherry glass	5. Seafood fork	9. Salad fork
2. White wine glass	6. Soup spoon	10. Dessert fork and spoon
3. Red wine glass	7. Dinner knife	11. Butter plate
4. Water goblet	8. Dinner fork	

Formal Table Setting

6.2 Western Cuisine

Generally there are six or seven courses at the most formal dinner. The first course is called an *appetizer*, which is a type of small snack before a meal, either hot or cold. Sometimes it can be shared. It mainly tastes salty and sour, e.g., stewed sausage with cream or fried herring with egg sauce.

Soup is the second course. Traditionally, soups are classified into two main groups: Clear soups and thick soups. Clear soups are combinations of

Lobster Bisque

vegetables, meat, grains or pasta floating in a clear broth. Thick soups are classified depending upon the type of thickening agent used: *Purées* are vegetable soups thickened with starch; *bisques* are made from puréed shellfish or vegetables thickened with cream; *cream soups* may be thickened with béchamel sauce, etc. Sometimes soups are served below the room temperature, which are known as cold soups. Cold soups are a particular variation on the traditional soup, e.g., cucumber soup or cold borscht (based on beets).

Then follows the *side dish*, which will be taken as the third course. Since sea fish is easy to digest, it often goes before the main course. If seafood is served as the second dish, side dishes may be omitted or replaced.

The *main course* comes next, which is mainly made of beef, mutton, or pork. Roasted, fried and grilled are the usual ways to prepare the main course.

The fifth course is a *vegetable dish* or *salad*. It is any of a wide variety of dishes including green salads and other salads. Green salads include leaf lettuce and vegetables with a sauce or dressing. Other salads are based on pasta, noodles, or gelatin. Most salads are traditionally served cold. This course can be either after or with the main course. If you're dining American style, the salad comes out before the main course.

Spinach and Potato Puree

The *dessert* is a course that typically comes after the main course, usually consisting of pudding, cakes, ice cream, cheese, fruit, etc.

A cup of coffee or tea will be offered as the last dish.

If you order for yourself at a restaurant, what you need to decide first is the main course. You don't need to order all the courses unless you have a very good appetite and are sure to be able to eat them all up.

6.3 Napkin Etiquette

Wait for the host or hostess to take his or her napkin off the table and place it in his or her lap. It is a signal that the meal is about to begin. Unfold your napkin in one smooth motion without "snapping" or "shaking" it open and place it in your lap. An exception to this rule is buffet-style meals, where you should unfold your napkin when you start eating.

Don't tuck a napkin into your collar, between the buttons of your shirt, or in your belt. The size determines how you unfold a napkin in your lap. Large napkins provided at more formal dinners, are folded halfway. Smaller napkins are unfolded completely and fully cover the lap.

If a napkin ring is present, remove your napkin and place the ring to the top-left of the setting.

At the end of the meal, grasp the napkin in the center, pull it through the ring, and lay it on the table with the point facing the center of the table.

During the meal use your napkin frequently to dab the corners of your mouth. Cover your mouth with the napkin if you burp. Quietly say "Excuse me" but to no one in particular.

If you need to leave the table during the meal, place the napkin on the chair and slide the chair under the table. If the chair is upholstered, place the napkin soiled side up. At the end of the meal, the napkin is loosely folded on the table. If a plate is in the center of your place setting and when leaving the table, lay the napkin to the left of the plate. If the center of your place setting is empty, the napkin is laid in the middle of the place setting. Leave your napkin in loose folds that keep soiled parts hidden. If after-dinner coffee is served at the table, the napkin remains in the lap.

6.4 Table Manners

6.4.1 Posture

Proper posture at the table is very important. Sit up straight and try not to lean on the table. Never slouch or tilt back while seated in your chair. Keep your elbows off the table and close to the body when you are eating. However, when you stop to talk, it is okay to rest your elbows on the table and lean forward. It is permissible to lean forward slightly every now and then and to press the elbows very lightly against the edge of the table, if it is obvious that you are not using them for support.

When the knife is not in action, it is most pleasing to have the free hand resting on the lap, although few people will mind a forearm resting on the table. The eating arm should rise off the table when carrying food to mouth; the mouth must not be lowered to meet the fork or spoon. One leans slightly forward to avoid drips in one's lap. Silverware should not be waved around while one is talking.

6.4.2 Use of Silverware

The set of silverware facing you at a formal dinner can be difficult to handle, but the rule is simple: Use it from the outside in. Start with the knife, fork or spoon that is farthest from your plate. Use a soup spoon for soup. It's the spoon next to the knives on the right side of the plate. When the main course arrives, pick up the fork and knife closest to the plate. That knife is called the dinner knife, which is next to the soup spoon and closest to the plate. Cut meats in the main course with it. Your dessert silverware may be at the top of your dinner plate or appear with your dessert. There may also be a spoon for your coffee placed at the top of the plate with the dessert silverware.

Hold the knife in the right hand and the fork in the left hand (unless you're left-handed). There is a slight difference between American and European styles in using a knife and fork. In the European style, pick up the cut pieces of food with fork in your left hand, tines facing down, and the knife still in your right hand. While in the American style, move your knife to the top part of the dinner plate. Make sure that the sharp edge of the knife is facing in. Then change your fork from your left to your right hand, tines facing up.

You can rest your utensils in one of two ways when taking a break from eating. Put your fork and knife in the center of your plate with the tips facing each other in an inverted V (slightly angled); or rest your knife on the top right of your plate (diagonally) with the fork nearby (tines up). These two resting positions, recognized by trained wait staff, signal that you're not ready to have your plate removed. What's more, silverware should not touch the tablecloth once they are used.

If soup or dessert is served in a deep bowl, cup, or stemmed bowl set on another plate, place the used spoon on this bottom plate when you finish. If the bottom plate is too small to balance the spoon, the spoon is laid in the bowl. If the bowl is what is called a soup plate (shallow and wide), then leave the spoon in the bowl.

When you are done eating, place the knife and fork parallel with the handles in the four o'clock position on the right rim of the plate. The tips rest in the well of the plate in the ten o'clock position. The sharp edge of the knife should face inwards and the fork tines may be either be up or down. Make sure your silverware is in such a way that they won't slide off when the server removes the plate at the end of the meal.

6.4.3 Serving Food

Traditionally, dishes should be served from the left, and taken away from the right. However, wine and all other beverages are presented and poured from the right. This is logical, since glasses are placed above and to the right of the guest's plate, and trying to pour from the left would force the server to reach in front of the guest.

The informal dinner can be served as courses or with food heaped in bowls. Guests pass the bowls of food from one person to the next. The normal order is counterclockwise, or from left to right. This technique is a throwback from the times when dinner was served by waiters or a butler carrying a large tray.

Just how close does something on the table have to be before you reach out and get it yourself? That's simple: Within easy reach of your arms when you're leaning only slightly forward. Never lean across somebody else's plate. A request to "please pass the…" is required for everything beyond that invisible boundary, as is a "thank you" to whoever does the passing. Another point about passing is to always pass the salt and pepper together. If a person asks for just one, pass both anyway.

When using serving utensils, there are some general guidelines: Serving utensils are placed on the right side of dinnerware; when a serving spoon and serving fork are presented together, the spoon is laid on the right side ready to cut and lift while the fork is on the left side to steady and hold. The utensils are returned to the serving bowl in the same position. When a serving spoon is presented on a bottom plate and is used, the utensil is replaced in the bowl (ready for the next person to use).

6.4.4 Having Soup

Having soup politely and without fuss can pose challenges even to those well skilled in all forms of etiquette. Pay careful attention when eating in order to be polite and considerate to those around you.

When soup is served, look for a spoon. There should be at least one by your plate. If you have two spoons, the soup spoon is the larger of the two. If the soup served is initially too hot, let it cool. Avoid blowing on top of it. You can stir it slightly with your spoon to help cooler air move through the body of the soup.

Dip the spoon into the soup while moving it away from your body, until it is about two-thirds full, then sip the liquid from the side of the spoon, not the end. The theory behind this is that a diner who scoops the spoon plate-away, not toward himself, is more likely to slosh soup in the bowl, therefore not on his lap.

Use your spoon to eat the last drop of soup. Do not lift the bowl up and tilt towards your mouth to catch any liquid that remains. Do not make slurping sounds when eating. Place the spoon on the side of the bowl with a gentle motion to avoid making unpleasant noises.

6.4.5 Manners of Eating

Eating manners are very important since it is repeated many times every day. It must be done properly whether eating alone, with family, or with friends. You should train yourself in proper eating manners, if alone or with others. It will then become a natural part of your behavior, and you will be at ease at the table.

Once you start to eat, don't literally bite off more than you can chew: Take a manageable bite, chew it well, and swallow it before taking another. Close your mouth while eating to avoid unnecessary noises. When you have a mouthful of food, avoid doing two more things: Taking a drink and talking. If you have more than a few words to say, swallow your food, rest your fork on your plate, and speak before you resume eating.

It is preferred that eating should not be done in silence. It is good manners to talk during meals. Topics should be nice stories suitable for eating. Take turns during the conversation.

Eat at a relaxed pace when dining with others. Pace yourself to match your fellow diners. Correctly, no one should start eating until everyone has been served. However, if some people are served before others, those not served should turn to those who are served, and say "Don't wait; please start." The served do so, but pick slowly at their food so that the others will be able to catch up.

6.4.6 Manners of Drinking

Drinking manners are no less important. Do not pour your drink down your throat in one gulp. Drink it in several sips. Gently dab your mouth with the napkin before taking a drink. This prevents crumbs from falling into your glass. Do not breathe out in your glass. This will irritate others and will smudge the glass or the cup. Do not drink directly from the bottle. Besides being an unhealthy behavior, others who may want to drink after you could be irritated.

When it comes to wine: At a simple meal where one wine is served, choose a wine that best compliments the main course. When two wines are served, serve in the following order: Sparkling wines before still wines, white wines before red, light wines before heavy, dry wines before sweet and ordinary wines before fine. Food is the real determining factor though. The most important goal is to choose the wines that best suit your menu and serve them in that order. Red wines are usually paired with red meat, such as beef. White wines are usually paired with white meat, such as chicken or pork.

There are subtle differences between wine glasses used for red wine and white wine. A traditional red wine glass has a bowl wide enough so that it may be cupped in the hand, allowing the wine to be subtly warmed by your palm. This large bowl also allows you to swirl the wine and sample the bouquet, which is concentrated around the rim of the glass.

White wine glasses have a longer stem and more slender globe than red wine glasses. The longer stem keeps your fingers away from glass so that the wine stays as cool as possible. The slender globe helps maintain the wine's liveliness.

Champagne and other sparkling wines are served in glasses called "flutes" that have a narrow shape which helps preserve bubbles and direct them up the glass. Port is served in a small, slim tapered glass. While smaller than a wine glass, this glass is still large enough to swirl the port. Sherry is served in an even smaller narrow, tapered glass.

6.4.7 Forks or Fingers?

You use the fork even when facing a number of foods that easily could easily be eaten with the fingers. Generally, if something could grease up your fingers, don't touch it. The exceptions are French Fries, fried chicken, hamburgers and hot dogs. They may be eaten with fingers at a barbecue or fast food restaurant. Bread and some other foods such as raw vegetables, may be eaten with the fingers. With bread rolls, break off and butter one bite-sized piece at a time.

Fruits and berries on the stem may also be eaten with the fingers. For example, strawberries with hulls, cherries with stems, or grapes in bunches. Fruits such as apples, peaches, or pears can be cut into quarters, and then eaten with the fingers or dessert fork.

In the West, shrimp is mostly served in a glass known as a "shrimp cocktail" dish, consisting of shelled shrimps in a mayonnaise and tomato sauce. While eating, take the tail of shrimp with fingers and dip it in the sauce.

6.4.8 Other Table Manner Tips

Excusing yourself. When you need to get up to go to the restroom, it isn't necessary to say where you're going—a simple "Excuse me, please; I'll be right back" is sufficient. At other times, a brief explanation is preferred: "Please excuse me while I check with the babysitter." Leaving without a word is rude.

Burping, coughing, yawning, or sneezing at the table should be avoided. If you do so, turn your head from the table and say, "Excuse me."

Never answer the telephone at the table. If you need to take an urgent call, excuse yourself and go outside.

Removing unwanted food from your mouth. Food is removed the same way it went in—on silverware, i.e., by hand, by fork, etc., with the exception of fish bones, which are removed from the mouth between the fingers.

To remove spoiled food, cover the mouth with one hand, remove it with the other hand, place it on the plate, and cover it with another portion of food (if possible). In a private residence, rather than embarrass the hostess by telling her that a particular dish contains foreign matter or is tainted, eat from the unspoiled portion. But if this is not possible, move the portion around on the plate so it looks as if you are eating, and leave the tainted part alone. In a restaurant, tell the server so he or she may make a replacement.

Something caught in your teeth. Never pick food out of your teeth with your fingernails. A toothpick is also an offensive sight in operation. When food is caught between the teeth that is annoying or uncomfortable, wait to remove it privately.

6.5 Seating Arrangements

In western countries, people usually use long, rectangular, or oval tables. The traditional way of assigning seats at a dinner party is with place cards. They indicate guest seating in a subtle way without a lot of verbal instructions from the host. If there are more than six guests, the hosts will write the full name of each guest in an elegant print on the cards.

There are some basic rules for the table. When the dinner party has two hosts, then they will sit at opposite ends of the table in order to share themselves around a little bit more to their guests. The hostess is normally seated at the head of the table, while the host sits at the foot of the table.

If you have a guest of honor, for example, a boss, or an elderly relative, there are rules of etiquette as to their seating. A female guest of honor would normally sit to the right of the host, whereby a male guest of honor would normally sit to the left of the hostess. This is because the right side seat is always regarded as the honored one and "ladies first" principle applies to the case as well. Alternatively, the guests of honor can be placed at the opposite end of the table to the hosts. For a female guest of honor, place her opposite the hostess and for a male guest of honor, place him opposite the host. The remaining host can be placed next to the guests of honor.

It is also customary to alternate male and female guests in many cultures. Some business dinners are seated male-male-female-female for variety. Guests with partners are usually seated opposite each other. But if it is a round table, partners might be seated side by side. Children should always be seated with their parents.

6.6 Going Dutch

Among friends, going Dutch at a restaurant is a fairly common practice in western countries. Unless it was made very clear that someone else is paying, you are expected to pay your share of the bill except when you are on a date. It is widely accepted that on a date, the man should be the one taking the initiative when it comes to paying the bill, which means that he is the one to pay, unless the woman signals that she will cover the tab, after which it becomes impolite for the man to insist on paying; it shows respect for the woman's desire to be treated equally to let her pay the bill.

If you are with friends, and someone else grabs the bill and says, "Here, I'll get this," you might protest, but you can generally assume that the other person really means to pay.

A frequent question is whether to have each person pay for exactly what he/she ate, or simply split the bill in equal shares. Actually, there are two possible senses of "Going Dutch"—each person paying their own expenses, or the entire bill being split (divided evenly) between all participants. In strict usage, "Going Dutch" refers to the former, paying one's own expenses, with the later being referred to as "splitting the bill," but in casual usage these may both be referred to as "Going Dutch." Splitting the bill is generally easier to calculate, as it does not require checking what each individual ordered, but has the downside that people who ordered more expensive items are subsidized by others, and may be encouraged to order more expensive items knowing that their costs will be subsidized. So the person who says, "Let's split it, shall we?" should not be the one who ate the most.

After paying your share of the bill, do not forget to leave a tip if necessary. The easiest solution is to split tip evenly. While some people do mind splitting the entire bill, most people do not mind splitting the tip evenly, since it is only a small percentage of the total bill. Collect a tip for the server and put it on the napkin or under the plate before leaving the restaurant.

◆ Vocabulary ◆

utensil /juːˈtensl/ **n.** an implement for practical use (especially in a household) 餐具

spreader /ˈspredə/ **n.** a small knife for spreading butter 涂抹黄油、果酱用的小刀

napkin /ˈnæpkin/ **n.** a small piece of table linen that is used to wipe the mouth and to cover the lap in order to protect clothing 餐巾

cutlery /ˈkʌtləri/ **n.** tableware implements for cutting and eating food 刀叉

roll /rəul/ **n.** small rounded bread either plain or sweet 小圆面包

sterling /ˈstəːliŋ/ **a.** highest in quality 标准纯度的

appetizer /ˈæpiˌtaizə/ **n.** food or drink to stimulate the appetite (usually served before a meal or as the first course) 开胃菜

sausage /ˈsɔsidʒ/ *n.* highly seasoned minced meat stuffed in casings 香肠

herring /ˈheriŋ/ *n.* valuable flesh of fatty fish from shallow waters of northern Atlantic or Pacific; usually salted or pickled 鲱鱼

pasta /ˈpɑ:stə/ *n.* shaped and dried dough made from flour and water and sometimes egg 意大利面食

broth /brɔ:θ/ *n.* liquid in which meat and vegetables are simmered; used as a basis for e.g., soups or sauces 浓汤

agent /ˈeidʒənt/ *n.* a substance that exerts some force or effect 药剂，作用剂

starch /stɑ:tʃ/ *n.* a complex carbohydrate found chiefly in seeds, fruits, tubers, roots and stem pith of plants, notably in corn, potatoes, wheat, and ric 淀粉

puree /ˈpjuərei/ *v.* rub through a strainer or process in an electric blender 做成酱或泥

béchamel /ˌbeiʃəˈmel/ *n.* a rich white sauce 贝夏梅尔调味白汁

borscht /bɔ:ʃt/ *n.* a Russian soup usually containing beet juice as a foundation 罗宋汤

beet /bi:t/ *n.* round red root vegetable 甜菜

lettuce /ˈletis/ *n.* any of various plants of the genus Lactuca 生菜

gelatin /ˈdʒelətin/ *n.* an edible jelly (sweet or pungent) made with gelatin and used as a dessert or salad base or a coating for foods 食用胶

tuck /tʌk/ *v.* fit snugly into 塞进

dab /dæb/ *v.* touch or stroke lightly 轻拭

burp /bə:p/ *v.* expel gas from the stomach 打嗝

upholster /ʌpˈhəulstə/ *v.* provide furniture with padding, springs, webbing, and covers 为……装上垫子(套子等)

soil /sɔil/ *v.* make soiled, filthy, or dirty 弄脏

slouch /slautʃ/ *v.* assume a drooping posture or carriage 没精打采地坐(或走、站)

forearm /ˈfɔ:rɑ:m/ *n.* the part of the superior limb between the elbow and the wrist 前臂

tine /tain/ *n.* prong on a fork or pitchfork or antler 尖头

diagonally /daiˈægənəli/ *ad.* in a diagonal manner 斜地, 对角地

rim /rim/ *n.* the shape of a raised edge of a more or less circular object (圆形物体的)边，缘

beverage /ˈbevəridʒ/ *n.* any liquid suitable for drinking 酒水，饮料

throwback /ˈθrəubæk/ *n.* a reappearance of an earlier characteristic 回归

bulter /ˈbʌltə/ *n.* a domestic worker in a large household 男管家

fuss /fʌs/ *n.* a rapid bustling commotion 忙乱

stir /stə:/ *v.* move an implement through with a circular motion 搅拌

scoop /sku:p/ *v.* take out or up with or as if with a scoop (用勺子等)舀，盛

slosh /slɔʃ/ *v.* spill or splash copiously or clumsily 泼，溅

slurp /slə:p/ *v.* eat noisily 出声地吃喝

gulp /gʌlp/ *v.* to swallow hurriedly or greedily or in one draught 大口吞

smudge /smʌdʒ/ *v.* make a smudge on; soil by smudging 留下污迹

compliment /'kɔmplimənt/ ***v.*** say something to someone that expresses praise 赞美

subtle /'sʌtl/ ***a.*** be difficult to detect or grasp by the mind 细微的

swirl /swə:l/ ***v.*** flow in a circular current, of liquids 晃动, 打旋

bouquet /'bukei/ ***n.*** a pleasingly sweet olfactory property (酒的)芳香

flute /flu:t/ ***n.*** a tall narrow wineglass 细长香槟杯(形似长笛)

port /pɔ:t/ ***n.*** sweet dark-red dessert wine originally from Portugal 波尔图葡萄酒

taper /'teipə/ ***v.*** give a point to (使)成锥形

sherry /'ʃeri/ ***n.*** dry to sweet amber wine from the Jerez region of southern Spain or similar wines
    produced elsewhere; usually drunk as an aperitif 雪利酒

barbecue /'bɑ:bikju:/ ***n.*** a cookout in which food is cooked over an open fire 烧烤

hull /hʌl/ ***n.*** persistent enlarged calyx at base of e.g., a strawberry or raspberry 花萼

mayonnaise /,meiə'neiz/ ***n.*** egg yolks and oil and vinegar 蛋黄酱

taint /teint/ ***v.*** contaminate with a disease or microorganism 使变质

rectangular /rek'tæŋgjulə/ ***a.*** having four right angles 长方形的

alternatively /ɔ:l'tə:nətivli/ ***ad.*** in place of, or as an alternative to 或者, 二者选一地

tab /tæb/ ***n.*** the bill in a restaurant 账单, 费用

grab /græb/ ***v.*** make a grasping or snatching motion with the hand 抓取

subsidize /'sʌbsidaiz/ ***v.*** support through subsidies 补贴

◆ **Exercises** ◆

Ⅰ. Translation

Directions: *In this part there are 10 words or phrases in English. Please translate them into
    Chinese.*

1. appetizer   2. main course   3. serving spoon

4. butter spreader   5. fork tines   6. napkin

7. dessert   8. buffet   9. guest of honor

10. go Dutch

Ⅱ. Blank filling

Directions: *In this part there are two short passages with several incomplete sentences. Please fill
    in all the blanks.*

Passage 1

The set of silverware facing you at a formal dinner can be formidable, but the rule is simple: use it from the _____ in. Start with the knife, fork or spoon that is _____ to your plate. Use a soup spoon for soup. It's the spoon next to the knives on the _____ side of the plate. When the main course arrives, pick up the fork and knife closest to the plate. That knife is called the _____, which is next to the soup spoon and closest to the _____. Cut meats in the main course with it. Your dessert silverware may be at the _____ of your dinner plate or appear with your dessert. There may also be a spoon for your coffee placed at the top of the plate with the dessert silverware.

Passage 2

There are subtle differences between glasses used for red wine and white wine. A traditional red wine glass has a bowl wide enough so that it may be _____ in the hand, allowing the wine to be subtly warmed by your _____. This large _____ also allows you to swirl the wine and sample the bouquet, which is concentrated around the rim of the glass.

White wine glasses have a longer _____ and more slender globe than _____ wine glasses. The longer stem keeps your fingers away from glass so that the wine stays as _____ as possible. The slender globe helps maintain the wine's liveliness.

III. Essay questions

Directions: *In this part there are two essay questions. Please write the corresponding answer for each question.*

1. When you want to take a break from eating at a classy restaurant, what will you do with your napkin and fork and knife? What if you finish a meal?

2. Suppose you and your spouse come across another American couple who are your friends on the street. You four have a nice chat and decide to have lunch together at a restaurant nearby. How will you figure out the proper seating if it is a long table? And how will you deal with the bill? List possible solutions.

Situational Dialogues

Dialogue 1

(Making a reservation)

Waiter: Princess Restaurant. Good morning! Can I help you?

Caller: Yes, I would like to book a table for four for the next Wednesday, December 23.

Waiter: Certainly, sir. What time do you like your table?

Caller: At 8:30 on the next Wednesday evening.

Waiter: May I have your name, sir, please?

Caller: Please book it under the name of Mr. Watson.

Waiter: So it's Mr. Watson, a table for four for the evening of the next Wednesday. You are coming at 8:30.

Caller: That's right.

Waiter: Thank you for calling us. We look forward to your visit,

服务员：公主餐馆。早上好，有什么需要？

来电者：是的，我想预定下周三 12 月 23 日四个人的位子。

服务员：没问题，先生。你想预定什么时候的位子？

来电者：下周三晚上 8:30。

服务员：请问先生贵姓？

来电者：请记在华生先生的名下。

服务员：好，华生先生，下周三晚上四个人的位子，将在 8:30 过来。对吗？

来电者：没错。

服务员：谢谢您的致电。期待您的光临。

Dialogue 2

(Ordering food)

Waiter: Are you ready to order or do you need a few more minutes?

Customer: May I have a menu?

Waiter: Certainly, sir.

Customer: I'll have the green peas, and make sure the beef is well-done.

Waiter: Yes, sir. What would you like to drink?

Customer: I'll have a Scotch on the rocks.

Waiter: What will you have for dessert?

Customer: What comes with the special?

Waiter: Ice cream, fresh fruit, or chocolate cake.

Customer: I think I'll have a chocolate ice cream.

Waiter: Yes, sir.

服务员：您是现在点餐还是待会儿再点？

顾客：请给我菜单好吗？

服务员：当然，先生。

顾客：我要青豌豆，而且牛排务必要烤熟。

服务员：好的，先生。你想喝点什么？

顾客：我要加冰的苏格兰威士忌。

服务员：你要吃什么甜点？

顾客：有什么特色的吗？

服务员：冰淇淋、新鲜水果和巧克力蛋糕。

顾客：我想要一份巧克力冰淇淋。

服务员：好的，先生。

Dialogue 3

(Talking about food)

Mrs. Smith: Mr. Zhao, I'm afraid I'm not a good cook. I hope you liked the dinner.

Zhao: Oh, it's wonderful. It must have taken you a lot of time to prepare so many courses.

Mrs. Smith: Well, it didn't take me very long. You see, we've got two ovens in the kitchen, and that saves a lot of time. Do you sometimes feel you miss Chinese food?

Zhao: No, not really. I often cook myself a Chinese dinner.

Mrs. Smith: Oh? Can you find the things you need in America?

Zhao: Oh, yes. In New York at least, you can find almost everything you can think of. And there is probably a greater variety here than what I'm used to at home in the Chinese markets.

Mrs. Smith: Isn't that surprising? I hear Chinese food is very different from our Western food.

Zhao: That's true. In the West, people like to bake or roast, while in China we like to fry or stir fry.

史密斯太太：赵先生，恐怕我不是个好厨师。希望你能喜欢这顿晚餐。

赵：噢，非常棒。准备那么多的菜占用了你很多时间吧？

史密斯太太：没有。你看，我们厨房里有两个炉子，这样就节约了好多时间。你有时想念中
　　　　　　国菜吗？

赵：不，不十分想。我常常自己做中国菜。

史密斯太太：噢？你能在美国找到你需要的东西吗？

赵：是的。至少在纽约，你可以买到几乎所有你想要的东西。这儿的花样比过去我在中国市
　　场见到的可能还要多。

史密斯太太：这不令人吃惊吗？我听说中国食品很不同于我们西方食品。

赵：是的。在西方，人们喜欢烧、烤，而中国人常常煎、炒。

中国的菜系及特征

The History of Table Manners
By Jonathan Jones

Mealtime etiquette has relaxed hugely since Mrs Beeton's time. Do manners still matter?

In a painting by the 18th-century French artist Chardin, two young children are sitting down to eat. Their table is set in the kitchen of a great house, with pots and pans hanging on the walls, but it is elegantly laid. There is a cloth on the table, and two grand chairs for the children to sit at as they use their silver cutlery under a maid's supervision. It is 1740, and they are learning to eat. Or rather, they are learning table manners.

Where does food end and etiquette begin? Table manners define the meaning of a meal. Eating is a physical need, but meals are a social ritual. The 150th anniversary of Mrs Beeton's book *Household Management* this autumn draws attention to this weird (古怪的) and wonderful world of manners. In many ways it is a very modern book: Mrs Beeton's recipes and kitchen tips are the kind of thing you still get in cookery books today. Maybe her language is a bit clinical (严肃的, 客观的): There's a chapter on how to cook "quadrupeds" (四足动物). But the one thing that truly places the book in the past is its advice on table manners.

At a dinner party, "the lady begins to help the soup…commencing with the gentleman on her right and on her left, and continuing in the same order till all are served. It is generally established as a rule, not to ask for soup or fish twice, as in so doing, part of the company may be kept waiting for the second course." The complex rules set out by Mrs Beeton still exist (at a formal hall high table at an Oxbridge college, say), but even at the smartest restaurants, the rigorous (严格的) order of Mrs Beeton's dining table is rarely preserved nowadays.

It was, in fact, the culmination of hundreds of years of changing manners. The children learning their table etiquette in Chardin's 1740 painting are in the avantgarde (先锋的) of a cultural revolution. Cutlery, as opposed to eating with your fingers; sitting up straight in a high-backed chair; these were innovations in the way people defined themselves at table in 18th-century Europe. New meals were even invented specifically as occasions for polite manners: The English tea time dates from the 1700s and is richly illustrated in paintings by Hogarth and Devis. They show the stylised rituals of pouring the tea and holding the delicate porcelain (瓷) cup.

Europeans in the middle ages had had little ceremony when it came to food. Their manners consisted of making sure they didn't get too greasy (when tearing meat with their fingers. Chaucer's 14th-century *Canterbury Tales* portrays an elegant prioress (女修道院院长) as a mistress of medieval manners, "At meat well y-taught was she withal; She let no morsel from her lips fall, Ne wet her fingers in her sauce deep; Well could she carry a morsel and well keep; That no droppe ne fell upon her breast."

This is the height of British table manners five centuries before Mrs Beeton. And Chaucer, of course, is laughing at this over-refinement.

Go back thousands of years to the early Homo sapiens who lived at Cheddar Gorge, and gnawed (缺刻状的) bones found in the cave suggest the kind of mealtimes that were enjoyed here. Oh, some of those gnawed bones are human by the way. And a cup formed from a human skull has also been found.

The rich courtly gear of a Saxon king found at Sutton Hoo, meanwhile, includes a massive cauldron (大锅) and drinking horns, suggesting the importance of feasting to our ancestors. But there is nothing to indicate any refinement—there is no Sutton Hoo toothpick (牙签). Only in Renaissance Europe do paintings and artifacts (人工制品) reveal the dawn of table manners: just to contemplate (深思) the extreme beauty and fragility of a 16th-century Venetian (威尼斯的) wine glass is to realise how sophisticated the parties were where such miraculous ware was used.

Today, it might seem as though we have returned to the sloppiness (马虎) of medieval feasting, or even Cheddar Gorge. Barbecued wings and legs eaten with your hands, burgers, crostini (烤面包), pizza. The finger foods of the world merge in a great casual banquet, often eaten in front of the TV. Only at restaurants is some semblance (类似) of high dining still maintained. And yet, in truth, the rise of table manners shapes our lives as firmly as it did those children painted by Chardin. We still see straight-backed chairs and laid-out cutlery as essential to a "proper" meal. We still drink out of individual glasses. We may go to Starbucks instead of rushing home for a traditional English tea, but the consumption of a latte (拿铁咖啡) is a stylised act.

As Mrs Beeton said, all creatures eat, but "man only dines." Etiquette changes radically (彻底地) but it always exists. In manners as in recipes, we are not so far as we might think from her well-regulated world.

Chapter 7
Dressing Etiquette

着装礼仪

在本章中，你将了解到：
- 西方人的正装
- 商务套装
- 商务休闲装
- 休闲装

Intensive Reading

7.1 Formal Wear

Formal wear is the general term for clothing suitable for formal social events, such as a wedding, a formal garden party or dinner, the Opera, débutante balls, a dance, or a race. The Western style of formal evening dress, characterized by black and white garments, has spread through many countries; it is almost always the standard formal social dress in countries without a formal national costume.

The formal dress standards for the 21st century constitute formal and semi-formal dress. The dress code considered formal in the evening is *white tie* while *black tie* is considered semi-formal. *Morning dress* is the daytime formal dress code while *stroller* or *business suit* is semi-formal daywear. However, there has been a relaxation regarding the dress codes. The full formal dress (white tie or morning dress) is almost unheard of in many places, particularly in America, as well as around the Western world.

7.1.1 Morning Dress

In the UK, morning dress is standard formal daytime clothing, but in the US and Canada morning dress is rare. Morning dress, however, does remain in certain settings in Europe and Australia. Morning dress consists chiefly for men of a morning coat, waistcoat, and striped trousers. For women, it is an appropriate dress.

The standard components of morning dress for men consist of:

● a morning dress coat (the morning cut of tailcoat), black or Oxford grey with the tails of knee length, single-breasted with one (or very rarely two) buttons and with pointed lapels

● a pair of formal striped or checked trousers worn with braces (AmE. *suspenders*)

● a formal shirt with a tie

● a dove grey waistcoat (AmE. *vest*), sometimes buff, or at a funeral black

● black dress shoes with plain black socks

The following can optionally be worn or carried with morning dress:

● a top hat

● gloves of suede, the most traditional color is lemon or grey
● a cane or umbrella
● and a pocket watch on the waistcoat rather than at the lapel.

Morning Dress

7.1.2 White Tie

White tie is the most formal evening dress code in Western fashion. It is worn to ceremonial occasions such as state dinners in some countries, as well as to very formal balls and evening weddings. The chief components for men are the black dress coat commonly known as an evening tailcoat, white bow tie, white waistcoat and starched wing collar shirt. Women wear a suitable dress for the occasion, such as an evening gown. As evening dress, white tie is traditionally considered correct only after 6 pm, although some etiquette authorities allow for it anytime after dark even if that means prior to 6 pm.

Formal evening dress for men is strictly regulated, and properly consists of:

● a black or midnight blue dress coat (commonly known as an evening tailcoat) with silk facings, horizontally cut-away at the front
● trousers of matching fabric with one single wide stripe or two narrow stripes of satin or braid in the United States, two stripes in Europe; and are worn with braces
● a white plain stiff-fronted cotton shirt
● a white stiff wing collar, preferably detachable
● a white bow tie
● a white low-cut waistcoat (matching the bow tie and shirt)
● a black silk socks or stockings
● a black patent leather shoes
● a black silk top hat which may be collapsible
● and white gloves.

White Tie

Although female dress is not as formally codified as that of men, where white tie is prescribed, women are expected to wear the following components:

- a full-length dress, such as a ball gown (at the most formal balls, ball gowns are often required to be white. At hunt balls, ball gowns are often required to be black, white, silver, or gold.)
- jewelry—earrings and necklace; rings and bracelets are optional
- long gloves—if they are worn, they should be white and elbow-length and are never taken off until seated at a table (known as opera gloves).
- a shawl
- shoes—formal pumps or sandals
- a handbag—clutch style or small evening bag
- and state decorations—if they are worn, it will usually be appropriate for royal and aristocratic women to wear tiaras.

7.1.3 Stroller

The stroller or simply black lounge, is a form of men's semi-formal daytime dress. The term *stroller* is only used in the US and is unknown in the UK, where, though the garment itself saw a limited period of popularity and was simply called a *black lounge*. Since black was then reserved for formalwear, it was unknown as a color for lounge suits, so the term was clear. In the UK this mode of dress is now extremely unusual, though some Masonic Lodges which meet during the day rather than in the evening (as is more common) do continue to specify it as their dress code. It is also still worn within the legal profession, especially by barristers. In such a way, the striped trousers are in some circles referred to as "barrister trousers."

The components of the stroller consist of:

- a single/double-breasted suit jacket (grey or black)
- grey striped or checked formal trousers
- a dress shirt with a turndown collar
- a necktie (grey or silver)
- a waistcoat (dove grey, funeral black, or buff)
- and a boater hat.

Stroller

Opera Gloves

7.1.4 Black Tie

Black tie is also worn only to events after six o'clock in the evening. For a man, the main component is a usually a black jacket, known as a dinner jacket (in the UK) or tuxedo (mainly in the United States). The typical black-tie jacket is single-breasted, and black or midnight-blue. The double-breasted jacket is slightly more modern than the single-breasted jacket, and less formal. The white dinner jacket is often worn in warmer climates.

Women's dress for black tie occasions can vary to a much greater extent, ranging from a cocktail dress that is at or below the knee to a long evening gown, determined by current fashion, local custom, and the event's occasion.

Unlike white tie, which is very strictly regulated, black-tie ensembles can display more variation. In brief, the traditional components for men are:

- a jacket with ribbed silk facings on a shawl collar or pointed lapel

  (while a notched lapel is a popular modern choice, it is traditionally considered less formal)

● trousers with a single silk or satin braid covering the outer seams

● a black cummerbund or a low-cut waistcoat

● a white dress shirt and a turn-down or detachable wing collar (the latter are now more commonly worn for white tie, but are generally considered acceptable for black tie as well)

● a black ribbed silk bow tie matching the lapel facings

● shirt studs (optional, depending on the type of shirt) and cufflinks

● black dress socks, usually of silk or fine wool

● and black shoes—highly polished or patent leather shoes.

Black Tie

White Dinner Jacket   Cocktail Dress

In many cases, invitations will state the dress codes for the social events. If the invitation states: *Black Tie Preferred, Black Tie Optional* or *Black Tie Invited,* a traditional tuxedo is the preferred choice of attire for the gentleman. If he decides *not* to wear a tuxedo, he may wear a dark suit, white dress shirt and a conservative tie, which is the next step down from *Black Tie Preferred.* Anything less formal than this would be unacceptable at this event. If the gentleman does wear a tuxedo, then the lady accompanying him should be in a formal floor length gown. If the gentleman does not wear a tuxedo but a dark suit instead, a lady in this case will wear a short dinner gown or an evening suit, which is a skirt with matching jacket.

7.2 Business Attire

Business attire, also called *informal attire*, is more formal than *Casual* but less formal than *Semi-formal*. It is commonly worn in religious services, funerals, the government, schools, and other contexts where casual attire is not accepted, but formal attire would be considered excessive.

Business Attire

The major components of business attire for men consist of:

- a clean, pressed, solid-colored, conservative suit whose color varies from dark blue to gray or one in subtle pinstripe or plaid
- a long-sleeved, non-flashy shirt in solid colors such as white, cream or light blue
- a necktie in solids, stripes, or small patterns; and its tip should reach but not extend beyond the top of the belt
- and slip-on shoes or lace-up shoes in black or dark brown with dark or neutral color over-the-calf socks.

As for women, the strictest interpretation of informal attire (a suit consisting of a jacket with matching skirt or trousers) is not quite so commonly worn by women as by men, as there are other forms of female attire acceptable in informal settings. The major components are:

- a matched-skirted suit (the length of the skirt should be no shorter than slightly above the knee and no longer than just below the mid-calf) or a simple tailored suit or dress
- a blouse—if a suit is worn, it should be in solid colors or with simple patterns
- and leather pumps with neutral or nude colored hose or panty hose (the color of the shoes should match with the hemline or be darker than it).

7.3 Business Casual

Business casual is sometimes used interchangeably with the term *smart casual*, which is a loosely defined dress code. It is casual, yet "smart" (i.e., "neat") enough to conform to the particular standards of certain Western social groups. The function of smart casual dress is to make the person look well put together and professional, but in a slightly more relaxed environment.

Business Casual

Blazer

Men's business casual includes as follows.

● Tops: A long-sleeve dress shirt (tie optional); a polo shirt; a sweater; and if appropriate, a sport coat or blazer (with shiny, metal buttons)

● Pants: Khaki pants, dress slacks in linen or wool, jeans (if worn with a polo shirt or dress shirt), and a belt

● And shoes: Leather loafers or dressy slip-ons with dark, mid-calf socks.

Women's business casual includes as follows.

● Tops: A blouse or turtleneck, a jacket, a vest, or a sweater coordinated to the outfit

● Bottoms: Slacks or a skirt (long or short), a fashionable belt

● Shoes: Hoses or socks with boots, flats (leather, suede, or fabric) or mid-heel shoes

● And jewelry: Wear at least one coordinating piece—earrings, a bracelet or necklace.

A dress code is important because it suggests the mood that the organizer is trying to create at the event. At a work event, "business or smart casual" suggests that the event will be informal, but not inappropriately so. If the event is a wedding or a party, business or smart casual will create a relaxed, comfortable mood. However, it is still necessary to make an extra effort with your appearance. Dressing neatly and well will never come across as incorrect; just be careful not to appear too formal. Remember, this dress style is not a suit or evening gown; neither is it untidy sneakers or jeans.

7.4 Casual Wear

In daily leisure time without social events, one may wear anything he or she likes. Blue jeans and a T-shirt have been described as the "casual uniform." With the popularity of spectator sports in the late 20th century, a great deal of athletic clothes has influenced casual wear. Clothing worn for manual labor also falls into casual wear.

Skin exposure is most pronounced in casual wear, since it includes all swimwear, but the trend toward female exposure in the 21st century has also pushed the necklines of formal evening gowns ever lower and the skirts of semi-formal cocktail dresses ever higher. For men, the exposure of shoulders, thighs, and backs is still limited to casual wear.

Casual Friday is an American and Canadian custom which has spread to other parts of the world, wherein some offices celebrate a semi-reprieve from the constrictions of a formal dress code. During the rest of the week, business shirts, suits, ties, trousers, and dress shoes are the norm. On Casual Friday workers are allowed to wear more casual dress. Some companies allow jeans, T-shirts, and sneakers; but others require business casual or smart casual dress.

In the West, people always attach much importance to dress etiquette, that is, they know what is appropriate to wear on occasion and dress according to the dress code. In addition, there are some unwritten rules in everyday life. For example, never meet your guests in pajamas or wear pajamas to the supermarket or anywhere else other than your home; do not wear the same clothes two days in a row, take off your coat and hat after entering someone's house, etc. Following dress etiquette, even for the highly civilized individual, is a good way to adhere to basic guidelines so that you always show up in the perfect outfit, without unconscious offense at others.

◆ Vocabulary ◆

débutante /ˈdebjutɔŋt/ *n.* a young woman making her debut into society 初进社交界的女子
garment /ˈgɑːmənt/ *n.* an article of clothing 服装
costume /ˈkɔstjuːm/ *n.* the attire characteristic of a country or a time or a social class 服装，装束
stroller /ˈstrəulə/ *n.* a business suit consisting of a matching jacket and trousers 普通西装
lounge /laundʒ/ *n.* an article of clothing designed for comfort and leisure use 休闲装
tailcoat /ˈteilˌkɔut/ *n.* formalwear consisting of full evening dress for men 燕尾服
single-breasted /ˌsiŋgəlˈbrestid/ *a.* (of clothing) closing with a narrow overlap and fastened with a single row of buttons 单排扣的
lapel /ləˈpel/ *n.* lap at the front of a coat 翻领

striped /straipt/ *a.* marked or decorated with stripes 带条纹的

checked /tʃekt/ *a.* patterned with alternating squares of color 方格图案的

brace /breis/ *n.* elastic straps that hold trousers up (usually used in the plural) 背带

buff /bʌf/ *a.* of the color of buff leather 浅黄色的

suede /sweid/ *n.* leather with a napped surface 绒面革

cane /kein/ *n.* a stick that people can lean on to help them walk 手杖

starched /stɑːtʃt/ *a.* being stiffened as if with starch 浆得硬挺的

dress /dres/ *a.* suitable for formal occasions 适合正式场合的

satin /ˈsætin/ *n.* a smooth fabric of silk or rayon 缎子

braid /breid/ *n.* trimming used to decorate clothes or curtains 镶边

stiff /stif/ *a.* (of a collar) standing up rather than folded down （领子）直立的

detachable /diˈtætʃəbl/ *a.* designed to be unfastened or disconnected without damage 可拆开的

patent leather /ˈpeitənt ˈleðə/ leather with a hard glossy surface 漆皮

collapsible /kəˈlæpsəbl/ *a.* capable of collapsing or being collapsed 可折叠的

shawl /ʃɔːl/ *n.* cloak consisting of an oblong piece of cloth used to cover the head and shoulders 披肩

pump /pʌmp/ *n.* a low-cut shoe without fastenings 无带浅口鞋

clutch /klʌtʃ/ *n.* the act of grasping 抓紧

decoration /ˌdekəˈreiʃən/ *n.* an award for winning a championship or commemorating some other event 勋章

aristocratic /ˌæristəˈkrætik/ *a.* belonging to or characteristic of the nobility or aristocracy 贵族的

tiara /tiˈɑːrə/ *n.* a crown-like jewelled headdress worn by women on formal occasions 冠状头饰

Masonic Lodge /məˈsɔnik lɔdʒ/ *n.* a formal association relating to stonemasons or masonry 共济会

barrister /bæristə/ *n.* a British lawyer who speaks in the higher courts of law （可在高等法院出庭的）大律师

boater /ˈbəutə/ *n.* a stiff hat with a flat crown 硬平顶帽

ensemble /ɑːnˈsɑːmbl/ *n.* a coordinated outfit (set of clothing) 全套服装

ribbed /ribd/ *a.* (of the surface of shells) having a rough, rib-like texture 有棱纹的

cummerbund /ˈkʌməbʌnd/ *n.* broad pleated sash worn as formal dress with a tuxedo 宽腰带

stud /stʌd/ *n.* ornament consisting of a circular rounded protuberance 饰钉

cufflink /ˈkʌfliŋk/ *n.* jewellery consisting of one of a pair of linked buttons used to fasten the cuffs of a shirt 袖扣

pinstripe /ˈpinstraip/ *n.* having very thin stripes 细条纹

plaid /plæd/ *n.* a cloth having a crisscross design 格子花呢

solid /ˈsɔlid/ *a.* entirely of a single color throughout 纯色的

calf /kɑːf/ *n.* the muscular back part of the shank 小腿肚

hose /həuz/ *n.* stockings and tights collectively 长筒袜，裤袜

hemline /ˈhemlain/ *n.* the line formed by the lower edge of a skirt or coat （衣裙的）底边

blazer /ˈbleizə/ *n.* lightweight single-breasted jacket 单排扣外套

khaki /ˈkɑːkiː/ *n.* a sturdy twilled cloth of a yellowish brown color used especially for military uniforms 卡其布

linen /ˈlinin/ *n.* a fabric woven with fibers from the flax plant 亚麻布

loafer /ˈləufə/ *n.* a low step-in shoe 平底便鞋

slip-on /ˈslipˌɔn/ *n.* an article of shoe that is easily slipped on or off 便鞋

slack /slæk/ *n.* trousers especially for casual wear 宽松长裤

turtleneck /ˈtəːtlˌnek/ *n.* a sweater or jersey with a high close-fitting collar 高领毛衣

coordinate /kəuˈɔːdineit/ *v.* bring (components or parts) into proper or desirable coordination correlation 协调

outfit /ˈautfit/ *n.* a set of clothing (with accessories) 一套服装

neckline /ˈnekˌlain/ *n.* the line formed by the edge of a garment around the neck 领口

reprieve /riˈpriːv/ *n.* an interruption in the intensity or amount of something 暂缓

constriction /kənˈstrikʃən/ *n.* rules or factors which limit what you can do and prevent you from doing what you want to do 规定，限制

sneaker /ˈsniːkə/ *n.* a canvas shoe with a pliable rubber sole 运动鞋

pajamas /pəˈdʒɑːməz/ *n.* loose-fitting nightclothes worn for sleeping or lounging 睡衣裤

row /rəu/ *n.* a continuous chronological succession without an interruption 连续

◆ Exercises ◆

Ⅰ. Translation

Directions: *In this part there are 10 words or phrases in English. Please translate them into Chinese.*

1. white tie   2. black tie   3. morning dress

4. business suit   5. tailcoat   6. tuxedo

7. evening gown   8. cocktail dress   9. blouse

10. panty hose

Ⅱ. Blank filling

Directions: *In this part there is one short passage with several incomplete sentences. Please fill in all the blanks.*

The formal dress standards for the twenty-first century constitute formal and _____ dress.

The dress code considered formal in the evening is _____ while _____ is considered semi-formal. _____ is the daytime formal dress code while _____ or business suit is semi-formal daywear. However, there has been a relaxation regarding the dress codes, with full formal dress (white tie or morning dress) almost unheard of in many places, particularly in America, but also around the Western world.

III. Essay questions

Directions: *In this part there are two essay questions. Please write the corresponding answer for each question.*

1. Suppose you and your spouse got an invitation for a dinner party this evening. The invitation states "Black Tie Preferred." What will you and your spouse dress for the party? Try to explain it in detail.

2. In the Western terminology, is informal attire the same thing as casual attire? What are the differences between them?

Situational Dialogues

Dialogue 1

(Matching clothes)

Jane: I would like to wear this robe for tonight's cocktail party. What do you think of it?

Amy: Don't dress like that. You will make a fool of yourself. You look stupid in that robe.

Jane: What? But this is my favorite piece of clothing.

Amy: Maybe it is, but it's out of fashion.

Jane: What am I going to do?

Amy: Let's go downtown and pick out some fashionable clothes for you.

(In a clothes shop)

Amy: This purple shirt could match your handbag, don't you think?

Jane: Yeah, but I don't like purple. I have an eye on that long white dress.

Amy: But it is not for a cocktail party. It should be something special.

Jane: What do you think of the checkered shirt over there?

Amy: Marvelous. It will go with the party.

Jane: That's it. Need I take my handbag?

Amy: That's always necessary for ladies.

Jane: Which one shall I take?

Amy: The red handbag is much better than the blue one.

简：我想穿这件长袍去参加今晚的鸡尾酒会，你认为怎么样？

艾米：别那样穿。你会出洋相的。你穿那件袍子显得傻里傻气的。

简：什么？这可是我最喜欢的一件衣服。

艾米：或许吧。但它过时了。

简：那我怎么办呢？

艾米：让我们一起进城去为你挑几件时髦衣服。

(在一家服装店)

艾米：这件紫色的衬衫很配你的手提包，你认为呢？

简：是的，可我不喜欢紫色，我看中了那件白色长裙。

艾米：可它不适合参加晚会，你要穿得有个性一些。

简：你觉得那边那件格子衬衫怎样？

艾米：太妙了。参加酒会穿它再合适不过了。

简：就要它了。那我还带手提包吗？

艾米：对女士来说手提包是不可缺的哦。

简：那我该带哪一个呢？

艾米：红色的手提包比蓝色的更配你的衣服。

Dialogue 2

(Talking about clothes)

Tracy: Kitty, could you help me pick out an outfit to wear to work tomorrow?

Kitty: Sure, but why are you suddenly so serious?

Tracy: Well, tomorrow is the first day I work in the new department, and I want to make a good impression on everybody.

Kitty: I see. Are these two suits your choices to wear tomorrow?

Tracy: Yeah, but I can't decide which one is better.

Kitty: Well, what's your new position?

Tracy: District manager.

Kitty: So you need a high-powered image.

Tracy: Right. What do you think this black A-line dress with the caramel zip-front jacket?

Kitty: They are nice, but a little bit too girlish.

Tracy: What's your suggestion?

Kitty: If you really want to wear the A-line dress, you had better have this black 3-buttoned blazer over it.

Tracy: But don't you feel it's too dull? Everything is black.

Kitty: You can add a bright-colored scarf so you won't look too deathly black.

Tracy: All right.

崔西：姬蒂，可不可以帮我选一下明天上班要穿的衣服？

姬蒂：好啊！但你干嘛突然那么认真？

崔西：明天是我到新部门上班的第一天，我想给大家一个好印象。

姬蒂：知道了。这两套就是你明天准备要穿的吗？

崔西：是啊，但我无法决定哪套比较好。

姬蒂：你的新职位是什么？

崔西：区域部经理。

姬蒂：所以你需要一个高级主管的形象。

崔西：没错。你看这条 A 字裙配山羊绒拉链式夹克怎么样？

姬蒂：是不错，但看起来太小女孩子气了。

崔西：你建议怎么穿？

姬蒂：如果你一定要穿那条 A 字裙，那么最好配上这件有三颗扣子的黑色西装外套。

崔西：但是，你不觉得太暗淡了吗？全部都是黑色的。

姬蒂：你可以系一条色彩鲜艳的丝巾，这样就不会看起来一片死黑了。

崔西：好吧。

汉服

The History of the Opera Glove: From Josephine to Shania[1]

The Origin of the Opera-Length Glove

While gloves have been worn for nearly three thousand years, the garment we know as the

---

1 Much of the information was drawn from C. Cody Collins' 1945 book, *Love of a Glove* (Fairchild). This little book, is a veritable goldmine of information on gloves. Other sources of information used in this article include *Gloves*, Valerie Cumming (Anchor Press, 1982); *Hand In Glove*, Bill Severn (David McKay, 1965); and *Gloves Past and Present*, Willard M. Smith (Imperial, 1918).

opera glove seems to have first evolved in the late 16th and early 17th centuries. Queen Elizabeth I of England is reported as wearing an 18-inch-long pair of white leather gauntlets, with two inches of gold fringe, at a ceremony at Oxford in 1566. (Severn, p. 34) Some hundred years later, England's Queen Mary was painted in a portrait wearing a pair of elbow-length gloves (see the right picture).

Over-the-elbow gloves, as we know them, first became popular as standard items of fashion around the time of Napoleon I, though long gloves were already coming into fashion while he was still making his military reputation in Italy.

Napoleon himself was a great lover of gloves; he is reported, as of 1806, to have in his wardrobe (衣柜) no fewer than 240 pairs of gloves! He was very much appreciative of beautiful and interesting feminine attire, and encouraged his Empress, Josephine, and the other ladies of his court to dress in the height of style and fashion. For example, at his and Josephine's coronation (加冕礼) in 1804, the gloves made for the ceremony cost thirty-three francs per pair, a considerable sum in these days—but then, good gloves have always been costly! (Severn, p. 38)

The wearing of gloves by women had been popular since the time of Catherine de Medici, but the Empress Josephine, by her fancy for long gloves, started a nationwide craze, which rapidly spread throughout all Europe and America, during the Napoleonic period. [She actually wore gloves for somewhat prosaic (乏味的) reasons, since she was very dissatisfied with her hands, thinking them ugly; this is the same motivation that drove another famous beauty, Vivien Leigh, to wear gloves as frequently as she could.]

Napoleonic and Regency (摄政时期) (as this period was called in England—this was the era Jane Austen wrote about, and ladies wearing long gloves are often to be seen in films made of her books, such as *Sense and Sensibility* and *Emma*) gloves were of many materials and a bewildering variety of colors. Kidskin and cloth were favored materials, and the gloves were often made so that they fitted loosely around the wearer's arm and could be "scrunched" (皱紧) (down toward the wrist at the wearer's option).

Starting from about 1810, sleeves began to grow longer, and the length of gloves in most cases shortened correspondingly. However, long gloves were still customarily worn with formal dress until around 1825.

From approximately 1825 on, though, the opera glove fell

Josephine, then the wife of First Consul Napoleon, wears long gloves at a diplomatic reception

into a five-decade period of desuetude (废弃) as the long sleeves of the early- to mid-Victorian period came to dominate women's fashions; even when sleeves were worn short, as in most evening gowns of the period, gloves were still short, usually wrist-length, no more than 12 to 14 inches at most.

The Golden Age of the Opera Glove

The "opera glove," in the version we most commonly know it today—a glove of between 19 and 23 inches in length, made of kid leather and colored white, ivory or black, with a wrist opening closing with three buttons or snap, and often with three lines stitched (缝合) across the back of the hand—is a type called the *mousquetaire* in French. If that name sounds familiar when you sound it out, it should; the glove is a feminine adaptation of a style that was originally developed for use by the French musketeers (火枪手)—yes indeed, the Three Musketeers and that lot!—in the 17th century. In the original form, these gloves were made in singles (half-pairs) for use in dueling (决斗), and were constructed so as to fit over a sleeve. These gloves often had wrist belts with buttons for everyday dress and jeweled clasps for court wear. When the *mousquetaire* was redesigned for ladies, it was refined so that the glove was much longer (over the elbow usually, sometimes as far up as the shoulder), and designed with its modern characteristic feature, the lengthwise opening (usually 2 to 3 inches long), which is made to be closed with small buttons in clusters of three or four (most commonly of pearl or a pearl-like material), or, after about 1890, with snap fasteners. The longest *mousquetaires* were designed so that the sleeves could wrinkle attractively as they wrapped their wearer's arms. (Severn, p. 39, pp. 72-73) Before the 1870's, gloves tended to be

Sarah Bernhardt wears elbow -length white Mousquetaire gloves in one of her roles

wrist-length for daytime wear, since sleeves on daytime dresses were usually full-length in the Victorian period, and usually were elbow-length or shorter for evening wear. It is particularly appropriate that this site's gallery should feature so many actresses wearing gloves, for the *mousquetaire* was introduced to America during the 1870's by perhaps the greatest actress of them all, Sarah Bernhardt.

Mme. Bernhardt had rather thin arms (by the standards of those days), and the long *mousquetaires* she wore onstage flattered (使优点突出) her arms and hands perfectly, and drew attention to their expressive movements whenever she took the stage. Indeed, when she wore over-the-elbow gloves on one of her American tours, their beauty and elegance was so overwhelming to her audience that the *mousquetaire* almost immediately became universally accepted in America and Europe as a prerequisite for a lady's formal dress. (Severn, p. 39; Collins, pp. 73-74) (Mme.

Bernhardt, one of the great glove-wearers of all time, also was responsible for the popularizing of another important style, the four-button-length "slip-on" style.) The new style became immediately popular, ousting the previously universal short glove styles. The popularity of the opera glove/*mousquetaire* only grew through the remainder of the 19th century, hitting its peak in the Edwardian period.

A young woman in opera gloves, by Harrison Fisher

The illustrations of Charles Dana Gibson, Henry Hutt and Harrison Fisher are replete with pictures of beautiful ladies wearing kidskin opera gloves, almost universally white (white and its related colors, such as ivory, were considered the proper colors for gloves for formal occasions for many decades; black was considered a "daring" color, and opera gloves in other colors do not really seem to have started showing up until the 1920's or 1930's). Fisher, in particular, delighted in painting portraits of beautiful women in long gloves, as can be seen from this fine example of a contemplative young lady (see the top right picture).

In the Victorian and Edwardian periods, it was considered absolutely essential for a lady or gentleman to keep their gloves on at all times, even when bathing, and kid gloves were supposed to be skintight to a degree that would impress a modern-day fetishist (恋物癖者). In fact, gloves in the Victorian period were so skintight that ladies were unable to button their *mousquetaires* without assistance, hence the invention of the buttonhook! It was, in fact, considered improperly alluring (诱惑的) for women to put on or entirely remove opera-length gloves in public, and several etiquette writers of the time advised women to put on their long gloves at home before venturing outdoors. The button- or snap-fastened wrist opening which is the characteristic feature of the *mousquetaire* was put to very good use in this respect by many ladies of the period, who would slip their hands out through the opening to eat or drink while keeping the glove itself on. Harrison Fisher's painting of a young woman at tea demonstrates this custom in action.

The kid opera glove has become one of the items of clothing, next to the button-up shoe, that is most associated with the elegance of the late Victorian and Edwardian eras. Currently, though, long white opera gloves are most closely associated with

Kate Winslet's role in the 1997 movie *"Titanic;"* she wears kidskin opera gloves during a key dinner scene in the film, as the photograph below shows.

It is difficult, again, to overemphasize the importance of the glove to feminine fashion in this period of history. Gloves are, and were, so much associated with elegance and high class that they were worn on all possible occasions, from weddings to funerals. Indeed, speaking of funerals, it was for centuries a common custom for distinguished personages (名人), male and female, upon their deaths to be laid out and buried wearing gloves. This custom survived into the early 20th century.

Even to this day, the custom of "funeral gloves" (as Collins calls them in her excellent little book) survives with the presentation of gloves to pallbearers in many funerals. On a happier note, it is also still customary, at many weddings, for the bride and groom to give pairs of gloves to their attendants. This, in itself, is a survival of a very old custom from the times when gloves were quite expensive and were considered to be extremely significant symbolic gifts of love and friendship.

Opera Gloves in the 20th Century

In the Golden Age of Hollywood, very few actresses (being well-brought-up, even if they did get up to all sorts of hijinks [狂欢作乐]) would be caught dead on the street without their gloves. Attitudes toward gloves varied, of course.

While the wearing of gloves, as an indispensable part of a woman's outfit, fell into desuetude during the 1960's, opera gloves still pop up whenever a woman wants to look elegant or sexy. For example, country singer Shania Twain set the 1999 Grammy awards ceremony on its ear when she performed in an outfit that included shoulder-length, fringed black opera gloves.

To this day, actresses, singers and celebrities carry on the grand tradition of elegance and romance by wearing opera gloves!

Kidskin is an extremely soft, smooth, thin type of leather, made from the skins of milk-fed baby goats (kids). These kids are carefully raised so that they do not eat herbage (牧草) (which will change the texture of the skin in undesirable ways), or get bruised or scratched, so that their skins remain perfect and smooth. Kid leather is used for fine-grained, glace-finished (that is, grain finishing, a process in which a smooth, shiny finish is made on the topside of the skin by soft buffing or polishing on plush wheels) gloves, and kid gloves are often dyed so that the inside of the glove remains white. The traditional color for the kid glove—the default (默认) color, as it were—is white or some other related shade like ivory or taupe (灰褐色), and this color was and is especially favored for formal wear, but other colors, such as black, red, blue and brown have also found favor.

Chapter 8
Wedding Etiquette

婚俗礼仪

在本章中，你将了解到：
- 婚礼之前的序曲及宾客礼仪
- 西方传统婚礼、婚宴及宾客礼仪
- 赠送结婚礼物的礼仪

Intensive Reading

8.1 Before the Wedding

8.1.1 Engagement Party

Some engagements are announced at an *engagement party*. Traditionally, the bride's parents host the engagement party, but many modern couples host their own celebration and in some cases the event is planned by the future groom (bridegroom) to make the proposal to his intended bride.

Originally, engagement parties were normal parties at which a surprise announcement of the engagement was made by the father of the bride to his guests. The engagement party was to share the engagement news with family members and friends. Therefore, it was not a traditional gift-giving occasion, as none of the guests were supposed to be aware of the engagement until after their arrival.

In modern times, engagement parties often celebrate a previously publicized engagement. Gifts are often given and toasts or speeches are often made. Some couples choose not to have an engagement party.

While it varies, an engagement party is sometimes thrown at the beginning of the wedding planning process. For those with especially long engagements, engagement parties are held one to three months after the engagement, and/or about a year before the wedding. For others it can be held any time more than 6 months before the wedding. Since an engagement party is a more intimate affair, guests are generally limited to nearest friends and family who will be invited to the wedding; but that doesn't mean it should be the full wedding guest list.

An engagement party is often thrown at the couple's home or the home of a close friend or relative of the couple. This kind of engagement party usually includes engagement party gifts for the couple which are similar to wedding gifts in that they are household goods which will help the couple start their life together, but are usually less expensive and less formal than the gifts a couple will receive at their wedding.

8.1.2 Bridal Shower

A bridal shower is a gift-giving party held for a bride-to-be in anticipation to her wedding. The custom today is most common in the United States, Canada, and by American influence, in Australia.

The shower normally takes place 4 to 6 weeks before the wedding. Traditionally, hosting the bridal shower falls on the maid of honor. It is not proper for an immediate family member of the couple to host the shower. To do so would appear as if they were asking for gifts and is not in good taste. Guests are chosen from among the bride's personal friends, family, and other well-wishers. Women are usually the major participants at bridal showers. In general, people who are invited to a bridal shower are also invited to the wedding ceremony. Since every guest will bring a gift, it would be in very poor taste to ask someone to bring a gift for a bride who was not chosen to be invited to the wedding.

Showers are known as parties with a purpose. The purpose of a shower is to assist the couple in equipping their new home or for the bride to assemble a trousseau. Bridal shower invitations always introduce the theme or unifying element of the shower, such as kitchen showers, lingerie showers, etc. A shower invitation may also include a response card and a gift registry. A gift registry is a particular type of list of items the bride wishes to receive, which is made public and is limited to the stock of a given retailer. Traditionally, shower gifts are smaller and rather less expensive than wedding gifts.

Showers might be held at someone's house or a party room of a hotel. They are almost always informal gatherings with a simple menu and often only include cake, any type of food, or beverages. During the shower, games are played for fun and entertainment. The climax lies in the bride opening the gifts, reading the cards, and showing her gratitude to the senders in the presence of all the guests.

8.1.3 Rehearsal Dinner

A *rehearsal dinner* is a pre-wedding ceremony in North American tradition, usually held after the wedding rehearsal and the night before the wedding ceremony. The groom's parents are traditionally responsible for the financial obligation of the rehearsal dinner; however, any other close relative or friend may do the honor.

The purpose of the rehearsal dinner is for the relatives and friends of the bride and the groom to meet and have a good time. All attendants, the bride and her fiancé's immediate families, the officiant and spouse, as well as any out-of-town guests are included in the guest list. Family and friends of the bride or the host may also be invited.

The rehearsal dinner is usually held in a private home or a restaurant and is as formal or informal as the host would like, just so long as the wedding remains the main attraction. At some point during the evening, the best man offers a toast to the bride and groom. The groom then follows with a toast to his bride and her parents. The bride may follow with a toast her groom and his family. If the attendants' gifts have not already been passed out, now is the time to do so.

8.1.4 Other Tips Before Attending the Wedding

Respond promptly. Answer the wedding invitation before the R.S.V.P. date. It's best to confirm attendance a few days before the R.S.V.P. deadline, and proper etiquette suggests responding to the invitation in the manner requested. Even if you are not able to attend the wedding, it is still best to respond in a timely manner so that the couple will be able to get an accurate head count for the reception.

If you have declined the invitation, do not show up at the wedding. If you must cancel after you have accepted, do so as soon as possible. Additionally, don't bring a date unless your invitation specifically says their name or "+ Guest." Remember that the cost for each person attending a wedding is generally high so bringing unexpected guests is very impolite. This includes your children or other relatives.

Dress appropriately. When choosing the right attire for the day, adhere to the dress code. Most weddings are semi-formal, meaning you should choose a cocktail dress for evening and a short dress or suit for daytime. It is not considered proper etiquette to wear all white or black to a wedding, except for gentlemen who wear gentlemen's evening clothes. Do not wear caps or jeans except for a very informal outdoor gathering. If the wedding will take place in a church or chapel, wearing an outfit that does not show too much skin, i.e., arms, legs, or cleavage, is best.

8.2 At the Wedding

8.2.1 Wedding Procession

Arrive at the spot (usually a church) 15 minutes earlier so as to give yourself time to find a seat and get settled. If you are late and the processional or ceremony has already started, wait for a cue from the wedding coordinator. Ensure your mobile phone is off or on vibrate mode before you are seated. While the wedding procession starts, take the cue from the officiant about when to stand or sit. At most ceremonies, guests stand when the bride enters. Remain standing until the officiant asks you to be seated.

Wedding procession is one of the grandest parts of a wedding ceremony. The order of wedding processions follows a general pattern, but varies according to religious traditions. After all the wedding guests are seated, the mother of the groom and the mother of the bride are seated and the wedding ceremony begins.

The basic order of a typical processional is as follows:

The officiant, the groom, and best man typically enter by the side door and wait at the altar. They all stand facing the guests.

If there are more bridesmaids than groomsmen, the groomsmen (AmE. *ushers*) may also enter by a side door and take their places near the groom. Otherwise, they can escort the bridesmaids down the aisle. The best man should be closest to the groom.

The bridesmaids walk down the aisle at a slow and stately pace, beginning with the attendant who will be farthest from the bride. The maid of honor and/or matron of honor should be the last bridesmaid down the aisle.

The ring bearer and/or flower girl are next down the aisle. If there is one ring bearer and one flower girl, they may walk together, or if they will walk separately, the ring bearer will be first, followed by the flower girl. Ring bearers and flower girls are usually members of the bride's or groom's extended family. They are generally no younger than about 5 nor older than 10. The ring bearer carries a large white satin pillow on which imitation rings are sewn, while the real wedding bands are kept in the safekeeping of the best man. The flower girl may spread flower petals on the floor before the bride or carry a bouquet of flowers.

The bride is the last person to walk down the aisle. She may walk alone, though many brides choose to be escorted by their father, grandfather, brother, or another significant individual. After the bride has reached the altar, her escort may raise her veil if desired, or just hand the bride over to the groom. Once the escort is seated, the primary part of the ceremony can begin.

Ring Bearer and Flower Girl

8.2.2 Wedding Ceremony

Most wedding ceremonies involve an exchange of wedding vows by the couple, presentation of rings or other gifts, and a public proclamation of marriage by an officiant. Music, poetry, prayers, or readings from Scripture or literature are also optionally included in the ceremony.

The customary texts of traditional Roman Catholic vows are:

- *I, _____ , take you, _____ , to be my (husband/wife). I promise to be true to you in good times and in bad, in sickness and in health. I will love you and honor you all the days of my life.*
- *I, _____ , take you, _____ , for my lawful (husband/wife), to have and to hold, from this day forward, for better, for worse, for richer, for poorer, in sickness and in health, until death do us part.*

There is often the opportunity for the bride and groom to stamp their own mark on their Catholic wedding vows by exchanging the above promise to their spouse to be in a way personal to themselves. The priest will then say aloud, *"You have declared your consent before the Church. May the Lord in his goodness strengthen your consent and fill you both with his blessings. That God has joined, men must not divide. Amen."*

It is actually not proper for guests to take pictures at the wedding ceremony, especially if a photographer has been hired. Guests should arrange to purchase reprints from the photographer, and it's fine to take plenty of candid shots of the bride and groom and other guests after the ceremony has ended. Taking pictures during the reception is acceptable, even though a professional photographer may be present.

When the ceremony ends, guests should remain in their seats until the groomsmen dismiss them. If there are no groomsmen, be seated until mothers of the bride and groom have been escorted out. Allow family members of the bride and groom, who will be seated near the front, to exit first.

8.2.3 Wedding Reception

A wedding ceremony is often followed by *a wedding reception*. It is held as hospitality for those who have attended the wedding, hence the name *reception*: The couple receives society, in the form of family and friends, for the first time as a married couple. To be a reception, guests are usually greeted with a receiving line. In a receiving line, the wedding party, including the bridal couple, their parents, and any honor attendants, stand in order of precedence and greet every guest in turn.

Drinks, snacks, or often a full meal at long receptions are served while the guests and wedding party mingle. An elaborate wedding cake is popular in most western countries. In a symbolic cutting of the wedding cake, the couple may jointly hold a cake knife and cut the first pieces of the wedding cake, which they feed to each other. Then the cake is served to the guests.

As a guest at the reception, one should display courtesy and thoughtfulness. If a buffet is served at the reception, don't pile your plate full unless you are at the end of the line. You should be courteous of those who have yet to eat. Don't drink too much. You are there to celebrate with the newlyweds, not embarrass yourself and them. During the meal do not just talk to your date. Try to engage the people at your table in polite conversation even if you don't know them.

Either before or after food is served, the best man and/or maid of honor toast the newlyweds with personal thoughts, stories, and well-wishes; sometimes other guests follow with their own toasts. Champagne is usually provided for this purpose.

If there is dancing at the celebrations after the wedding, the newly married couple typically open the dancing with their first dance. After the first dance, the newly married couple might dance with their parents or new in-laws. Traditionally, shortly after the dance begins, guests would promptly join in the dancing.

A ceremony is often made of the newlywed's departure. Rice or birdseed, signifying abundance, may be thrown at the departing couple. The bride may toss her bouquet over her shoulder to a group of all the single women present, with folklore suggesting the person who catches it will be the next to wed. As the newlyweds are the guests of honor, the other guests are expected to remain at the reception until they leave them.

A modern tradition is for brides to wear or carry "*something old, something new, something borrowed, something blue*" during the service. It is considered good luck to do so. Often the bride attempts to have one item that meets all of these qualifications, such as a borrowed blue handkerchief which is "new to her" but loaned by her grandmother thus making it old.

8.3 Wedding Gift Etiquette

Traditionally it's no need for guests to bring their gifts to the ceremony. In some cultures (e.g., the UK), it is proper to send wedding gifts to the home of the bride and groom or to the home of the bride or groom's parents before the ceremony, although some couples may have a table set up in the corner at the reception for gifts. In other cultures (e.g., the United States), guests have up to one year to send their gifts. But waiting that long is extremely poor etiquette. One should send a wedding gift as soon as possible, preferably within three months of the joyful occasion.

It is appropriate to send a gift by purchasing an item from the gift registry and make selections based on your relationship with the couple, or give the couple cash as a gift, but it's best to present the money in check form. If you feel you'd like to give something that's not on the list, that's perfectly acceptable too. The registry is only a suggestion, and it's a bad manner for any couple to tell you specifically what gift to purchase or how much money to spend.

Even if a guest is not attending the ceremony or reception, it is still appropriate to send a gift to the newlyweds if he/she was invited to the wedding. If one has not received a thank-you note for their gift within two months, it's acceptable to write or call the bride or groom to ensure that the gift arrived safely. Other than that, it's considered tacky to discuss wedding gifts.

◆ Vocabulary ◆

bride /braid/ *n.* a woman participant in her own marriage ceremony 新娘

groom /gru:m/ *n.* a man participant in his own marriage ceremony 新郎

proposal /prə'pəuzəl/ *n.* an offer of marriage 求婚

toast /təust/ *n.* a drink in honor of or to the health of a person or event 祝酒词

intimate /'intimit/ *a.* marked by close acquaintance, association, or familiarity 亲密的

anticipation /æn,tisə'peiʃən/ *n.* pleasurable expectation 期盼

maid of honor an unmarried woman who attends the bride at a wedding 未婚主伴娘

well-wisher /wel'wiʃə/ *n.* someone who shares your feelings and expresses sympathy or hopes that something will be successful 祝福者

trousseau /'tru:səu/ *n.* the personal outfit of a bride 嫁妆, 妆奁

unifying /'ju:nifaiiŋ/ *a.* combining into a single unit 一致的

lingerie /lɑ:nʒə'rei/ *n.* women's underwear and nightclothes 女子贴身内衣或睡衣

registry /'redʒistri/ *n.* an official written record of names or events or transactions 注册

retailer /ri'teilə/ *n.* a merchant who sells goods at retail 零售商

rehearsal /ri'hə:səl/ *n.* a practice session in preparation for a public performance 排演

attendant /ə'tendənt/ *n.* someone who waits on or tends to or attends to the needs of another 服务人员, 随从

fiancé /fi:ən'sei/ *n.* a man engaged to be married 未婚夫

officiant /ə'fiʃiənt/ *n.* a clergyman who officiates at a religious ceremony or service 主婚人, 主祭

best man the principal groomsman at a wedding 主伴郎

accurate /'ækjurit/ *a.* conforming exactly or almost exactly to fact or to a standard or performing with total accuracy 准确的

decline /di'klain/ *v.* refuse to accept 谢绝

chapel /'tʃæpəl/ *n.* a place of worship that has its own altar 小教堂

cleavage /'kli:vidʒ/ *n.* the line formed by a groove between two parts (especially the separation between a woman's breasts) 裂缝; 乳沟

processional /prə'seʃənl/ *n.* a ceremonial procession 队列

coordinator /kəu'ɔ:dineitə/ *n.* someone whose task is to see that work goes harmoniously 协调者

vibrate /vai'breit/ *a.* characterized by vibration 振动的

grand /grænd/ *a.* lavish; wonderful 令人印象深刻的; 美妙的

altar /'ɔ:ltə/ *n.* the table in Christian churches where communion is given 圣坛

groomsman /'grumzmən/ *n.* a male attendant of the bridegroom at a wedding 男傧相

bridesmaid /'braidz,meid/ *n.* an unmarried woman who attends the bride at a wedding 女傧相

escort /'eskɔ:t/ *v.* accompany as an escort 护送, 陪同

stately /'steitli/ *a.* refined or imposing in manner or appearance 庄严的

matron of honor a married woman serving as the attendant to the bride at a wedding 已婚主伴娘

ring bearer one (usu. a boy) holding wedding rings at a western wedding 通常指在西式婚礼中拿戒指的男孩

pillow /'piləu/ *n.* a cushion to support the head of a sleeping person 枕头

sew /səu/ *v.* fasten by sewing; do needlework 缝

imitation /,imi'teiʃən/ *n.* a copy that is represented as the original 仿制品

petal /'petl/ *n.* part of the perianth that is usually brightly colored 花瓣

bouquet /'bukei/ *n.* an arrangement of flowers that is usually given as a present 花束

veil /veil/ *n.* a garment that covers the head and face 面纱

vow /vau/ *n.* a solemn pledge (to oneself or to another or to a deity) to do something or to behave in a certain manner 誓言

proclamation /,prɔklə'meiʃən/ *n.* a formal public statement 宣告, 声明

scripture /'skriptʃə/ *n.* any writing that is regarded as sacred by a religious group 经文, 圣典

Catholic /'kæθəlik/ *a.* of or relating to or supporting Catholicism 天主教的

stamp /stæmp/ **v.** reveal clearly as having a certain character 表示出, 使表明

priest /pri:st/ **n.** clergyman in Christian churches who has the authority to perform or administer various religious rites (基督教和罗马天主教的)神父, 牧师

consent /kənˈsent/ **n.** permission to do something 赞成

reprint /ri:ˈprint/ **n.** a reproduction of printed matter 翻印

candid /ˈkændid/ **a.** natural, especially caught off guard or unprepared 自然的，非故意摆出姿势的

mingle /ˈmiŋgl/ **v.** get involved or mixed-up with 混合

elaborate /iˈlæbəreit/ **a.** marked by complexity and richness of detail 精心制作的

courteous /ˈkə:tjəs/ **a.** exhibiting courtesy and politeness 彬彬有礼的

promptly /ˈprɔmptli/ **ad.** With little or no delay 迅速地，立即地

abundance /əˈbʌndəns/ **n.** the property of a more than adequate quantity or supply 大量，充足

toss /tɔs/ **v.** throw with a light motion (轻轻地)扔, 抛, 掷

folklore /ˈfəukˌlɔ:/ **n.** the unwritten literature (stories and proverbs and riddles and songs) of a culture 民间传说

tacky /ˈtæki/ **a.** tastelessly showy 低俗的

◆ Exercises ◆

Ⅰ. Translation

Directions: *In this part there are 10 words or phrases in English. Please translate them into Chinese.*

1. bridal shower
2. best man
3. maid of honor
4. wedding ceremony
5. wedding reception
6. officiant
7. groomsman
8. bridesmaid
9. ring bearer
10. flower girl

Ⅱ. Blank filling

Directions: *In this part there is one short passage with several incomplete sentences. Please fill in all the blanks.*

As a guest of a wedding ceremony, be sure to arrive at the spot (usually a church) _____ minutes earlier so as to give yourself time to find a seat and get settled. If you are late and the processional or ceremony has already started, wait for a cue from the wedding coordinator. Ensure your _____ is off or on vibrate mode before you are seated. While the wedding _____ starts, take the cue from the officiant about when to stand or sit. At most ceremonies, guests stand when the _____ enters. Remain standing until the _____ ask you to be seated.

When the ceremony ends, remain in your seat until the _____ dismiss you. If there are no groomsmen, be seated until _____ of the bride and groom have been escorted out. Allow family members of the bride and groom, who will be seated near the _____, to exit first.

III. Essay questions

Directions: *In this part there are two essay questions. Please write the corresponding answer for each question.*

1. What is a bridal shower? What are the major activities at a bridal shower?

2. Suppose you have received a wedding invitation from your American friend, but you find you cannot make it on that day. What would you do then? How would you deal with the wedding gift?

Situational Dialogues

Dialogue 1

(Wedding ceremony)

Judge: I think it's time for the wedding to begin. All right. Ladies and Gentlemen, please take your places. The wedding ceremony is about to begin. OK. Start the music.

(The music and ceremony begin.)

Judge: Dearly beloved, we are gathered here today to join this man and this woman in holy matrimony. Do either of you have any reason why you should not legally be joined in marriage? Is there anyone present who can show any just cause why these two people should not be legally joined in marriage? Then, Harry Bennett, do you take Mary Green to be your lawfully wedded wife?

Harry: I do.

Judge: And you Mary Green, do you take Harry Bennett to be your lawfully wedded husband?

Mary: I do.

Judge: The rings, please.

(Harry puts one ring on Mary's finger; Mary takes one ring and puts it on Harry's finger.)

Judge: By the power vested in me by the laws of the state of New York, I now pronounce you husband and wife. You may kiss the bride now, Harry.

(Harry lifts the veil and kisses Mary. The guests laugh, applaud and throw confetti.)

法官：我想婚礼应该开始了。好了，女士们，先生们，请大家各就各位，婚礼马上开始，请放音乐。

（音乐响起，仪式开始。）

法官：亲爱的朋友们，今天，我们在这里相聚，是这对男女结为夫妻。你们俩有哪位有理由说明你们不应结为合法夫妻的？在座各位有哪位有理由证明这两个人不能结为合法夫妻的？那好，哈里·班尼特，你愿意接受玛丽·格林为你的合法妻子吗？

哈里：我愿意。

法官：那好，玛丽·格林，你愿意接受哈里·班尼特为你的合法丈夫吗？

玛丽：我愿意。

法官：请交换戒指。

（哈里把一枚戒指戴在玛丽手指上，玛丽拿着一枚戒指给哈里戴在手指上。）

法官：用纽约州的法律赋予我的权力，我现在宣布你们结为夫妻。哈里，你可以吻新娘了。

（哈里掀开面纱，吻玛丽。来宾们欢呼鼓掌，抛洒五彩碎纸。）

Dialogue 2
(Discussing a wedding)

Julia: I would rather prefer an intimate affair with a few people...eh...where you really felt that it was a meaningful thing, and not just a showy, prestigious affair for...for the parents to show off what they can provide for their daughter or son.

Ray: But that's an important thing for the parents to do, isn't it? I mean, parents...it ought to be a ... parents ought to be allowed to do this.

Julia: But we are getting married, not my parents.

Ray: Yes, but if the parents are paying for it and if the parents who have, if you like, brought this young girl or boy up to...

Julia: Surely the money that is spent...I'd prefer to see the money is spent on something more worthwhile...

Ray: Yes, but it's not... it may not be your money as such. And I think if the parents are paying for it, then they should have a great deal to say in it. If they prefer to...to invite Aunt Flow and Uncle Bill who you haven't seen since you were two years old, well, I think that's their prerogative.

Julia: So it really boils down to what they prefer rather than what the son or daughter prefers...

Ray: Well, not entirely. Nevertheless I think it is important that they should...that they be consulted. After all, I think it's...it's as important a day for the parents as it is for... for the couple themselves.

Julia: Yes, I would agree, but I just think we have things that...have to be taken into account and the son or daughter's views should be solicited first rather than the parents' views.

Ray: They're very different, large weddings and small weddings, aren't they? In fact, weddings tend to commit to these two categories—very large or very small. Do you agree?

Julia: Yes, I...I prefer small ones, really. I think they're more genuine and more intimate. People really want to come, rather than people coming to stand around and criticize what you are wearing. That's not too pleasant, all this displaying of wedding presents so that you can see what so-and-so gave and compare them. I don't like that very much.

茱莉亚：我比较喜欢办一场只有少数人参加的私人婚礼，在那儿，你会真正感受到那是一件有意义的事，而不仅仅是一个奢华体面的场合，让父母可以炫耀他们为女儿或儿子所准备的一切。

雷：但这对父母来说也是一件很重要的事，不是吗？我的意思是，父母在这种场合下……这应该是……应该允许父母做这些。

茱莉亚：但结婚的是我们，而不是我们的父母。

雷：是的，但是如果是父母花的钱，这就可以。而且如果是父母把她或他抚养成人，如果你喜欢的话就可以……

茱莉亚：的确钱是花在了……我更愿意把钱花在一些更有意义的东西上。

雷：是的，但这不是……这不仅包含钱一方面。我认为如果父母愿意花钱，那么他们就应该有很大的权力管这事。如果他们喜欢大型婚礼，喜欢邀请弗罗姨妈、比尔叔叔这些你两岁以后就没再见过的人，那也是他们的权力。

茱莉亚：那这就归结于父母喜欢什么而不是他们的儿子或女儿喜欢什么。

雷：也不全是，但是虽然如此，和他们商量一下是很重要的。毕竟这对父母和这对夫妇来讲几乎是个同样重要的日子。

茱莉亚：我同意，但我认为有些事，应采取不同的视角，应先问下一下儿子或女儿的看法，而不是父母的看法。

雷：有许多不同的大型婚礼、小型婚礼，不是吗？事实上，婚礼无非分为两类——非常大型的或非常小型的婚礼。你同意吗？

茱莉亚：同意，我……我真的喜欢小型婚礼，我认为这更真诚、更亲切，人们是真的想来参加婚礼，而不是来冷眼旁观，评论你的衣着。婚礼所有的一切都是为了显示你的结婚礼物，来让你看到后进行比较，这是某某送的，这就不太好。我就不喜欢这种形式。

Supplementary Reading

中国婚礼习俗

The Latest in Wedding Rites—Bridal Showers for Men
By Candace Taylor

One of John Dixon's favorite wedding presents doesn't appear on most gift registries. In fact, before he got married last fall, Dixon, 34, had only a vague idea that laser levels—tools used for hanging pictures— existed.

Luckily, a family friend who has been married for 40 years brought the level to Dixon's "groom shower," where 15 men played poker, grilled hot dogs and presented Dixon with gifts they suspected he'd need as a husband.

Sure enough, Dixon has used the level four times since the wedding. "Suddenly my wife wants me to hang pictures," he said, adding that the shower was a unique opportunity for friends and family to give not only presents, but marriage advice.

Bridal showers have long been popular for women, but in recent years groom showers, often with sports or home-improvement themes, have become increasingly common. Experts say the trend is part of a broader tendency for grooms to become more involved in wedding planning than in years past, when such details were largely the domain of the bride and her mother.

"The wedding has always been about the bride," said Dixon, an elementary school physical education teacher in Happy Valley, Ore. "It's cool to have a piece of the wedding that's kind of the guys' chance to get together."

The popularity of groom showers is rooted in the fact that couples these days are more likely to plan and pay for their weddings, said Christa Vagnozzi, a senior editor at the wedding Web site—The Knot.

"Couples are more involved in the process now," Vagnozzi said.

Aaron Markson, 27, of Hudson, Wis., picked out the photographer and band for his nuptials last June. "It used to be that the girl made all the decisions, and the guy nodded his head," Markson said, "For our wedding, it was much more collaborative (协作的)."

This newfound (新发现的) enthusiasm has extended to pre-wedding festivities, prompting a rash (大量) of showers for couples and, increasingly, the grooms.

"My wife was having all these showers, and I thought, 'Why don't the guys get to do anything?'" said Markson, whose parents threw him a shower at their house in Brooklyn Park, Minn.

Groom showers are an outgrowth (自然结果) of the "gentleman's dinners" popular in the 1940s and 1950s, according to Bruce Vassar, one of the "Wedding Guys" who answer questions on the Web site TwinCityBridal.com. Usually hosted by the groom's father, such dinners functioned as "a dad's sendoff (欢送) to his son, to manhood and being married," Vassar said.

Over time, gentleman's dinners were largely replaced by wild bachelor parties, Vassar said. But in the past few years, more sedate (庄重的) sendoffs have resurfaced. Resembling "a much more tame version of a bachelor party," groom showers often consist of casual parties, trips to the racetrack (跑道) or rounds of golf, Vassar said.

Bachelor parties are still popular, but groom showers, or "power showers," function as an additional pre-wedding celebration for the groom's friends and family, he noted.

At Markson's bachelor party, for example, a few close male friends went jet skiing on Lake Minnetonka and barhopping (连着去几家酒吧) in downtown Minneapolis; his groom shower a few weeks later drew a very different crowd. At the shower, some 50 guests, including his mother, grandparents, uncles and co-workers, traded stories about Markson while scarfing (狼吞虎咽地吃) down his favorite foods: chicken wings and pizza with sausage and green olives.

"It was just a bunch of people coming together and hanging out," said Wes Wilmer, a pastor at the church where Markson is the music director. "It expands who's involved in their wedding at a deeper and more personal level than just the reception."

Groom showers aren't just for socializing. They also provide opportunities for the groom-to-be to stockpile (储备) "stuff that, as guys, we kind of want around the house," said Dixon, adding that the bride-to-be, despite having multiple showers, often selects most of the items on the couple's wedding registry. "Most of the things you register for, guys don't get that excited about."

Dixon threw his first groom shower 10 years ago, when he and a group of college buddies decided to hold a pre-wedding "tool party" for their friend Ethan. Guests brought toolboxes, work gloves and ladders to outfit the groom's new house—a fixer-upper (需要修缮的房子). Word of the successful event spread quickly, and groom showers became a tradition among Dixon's circle of friends.

But over the years, showers began to take on a greater significance for Dixon and his friends, evolving into a forum for advice as well as gifts. At Dixon's shower, he received an Xbox video game from a friend who told him, "You're going to need to lock yourself in a room sometimes and get away from it all." Another friend got him a "doghouse" kit, with items like massage oil for use when his wife, Jenessa, gets mad at him.

"It's a fun way of saying, 'Here are some of the experiences I've had,'" Dixon explained, "It's a show of support and encouragement from your friends."

Dixon believes that all this sharing and bonding—and men's greater involvement in wedding planning—has grown out of changing roles within the family. "Guys are allowed to be more sensitive than we used to be," said Dixon, who claims to cook more often than his wife.

Of course, this reimagining of gender roles is far from complete.

When asked about the dessert at his shower, Dixon said he and his friends usually avoid serving cake. Why? "It's not very manly," he said.

Chapter 9
Funeral Etiquette

丧葬礼仪

在本章中，你将了解到：

- 西方人的丧葬习俗及相关礼仪
- 参加葬礼的礼仪
- 其他表达悼念的方式

Intensive Reading

9.1 Funeral Customs and Etiquette

9.1.1 Condolence Visit

It is a common gesture for close friends of the bereaving family to visit the family's home to offer sympathy and assistance—this is referred to as a *condolence visit*. With the bereaving family having to ensure that all the arrangements are looked after, a close friend may become very helpful with food preparation and childcare. It's proper to bring a re–heatable dish or something. Chances are, cooking is the last thing on the bereaving family's mind. Besides, childcare assistance, transportation, cleaning or shopping help can also be offered to the bereaved. The visit can take place any time within the first few weeks of death, and may be followed with one or more additional visits, depending on the circumstances and your relationship with the family.

When a person visits the bereaved family's home, clasping hands, an embrace, or a simple statement of condolence, such as: "I'm sorry;" "I'm so sorry to hear of your loss;" "My sympathy to you;" "It was good to know John;" "John was a fine person and a friend of mine. He will be missed," can express sympathy. The family member in return may say: "Thanks for coming;" "John talked about you often;" "I didn't realize so many people cared" and "Come see me when you can." Encourage the bereaved to express their feelings and thoughts, but don't overwhelm them.

In addition to expressing sympathy, it is appropriate, if desired, to relate to family members your fond memories of the deceased. In some cases family members may simply want you to be a good listener to their expressions of grief or memories of the deceased. The kindest response is usually a warm hug and to simply say, "I understand." In most circumstances it is not appropriate to inquire as to the cause of death.

9.1.2 Visitation

In many cultures, the first event that follows a death is the viewing of the body, which is also referred to as a *visitation, calling,* or *wake*. It is typically held at the funeral home within a few days before the actual funeral memorial service.

Visitation provides a time and place for friends to offer their expression of sorrow and sympathy. The death notice will designate the hours of visitation when the family will be present and will also designate the times when special services such as lodge services or prayer services may be held. Persons may call at the funeral home at any time during the suggested hours of the day or evening to pay respects, even though the family is not present. *A funeral home* is a business that provides burial and funeral services for the deceased and their families. These services may include a prepared visitation and funeral, and the provision of a church for the funeral.

If you attend a visitation you should approach the family and express your sympathy. As with the condolence visit, it is appropriate to relate your memories of the deceased. If you were only acquainted with the deceased (and not the family) you should introduce yourself. It is customary to show your respects by viewing the deceased if the body is present and the coffin *(AmE. casket)* is open. You may wish to say a silent prayer for, or meditate about the deceased at this time. In some cases the family may escort you to the coffin. Your presence at the visitation demonstrates that although someone has died, friends still remain. Your presence is an eloquent statement that you care.

Normally visitors are requested to sign the register book. A person's full name should be listed, e.g., "Mrs. John Doe." If the person is a business associate, it is proper to list their affiliation, as the family may not be familiar with their relationship to the deceased. Colleagues and co-workers of the deceased may attend calling hours together, but try not to descend on the bereaved all together. Offer individual sympathy and a word or two of support. The length of your visit at the visitation is a matter of discretion. After visiting with the family and viewing the deceased you can visit with others in attendance.

9.1.3 Funeral Dress Codes

Nowadays, funeral dress codes have relaxed somewhat. Black dress is no longer required. Instead subdued or darker hues should be selected, the more conservative the better, especially if there is a religious service at a church, funeral home or grave side. Black, navy, gray, or other dark colors usually appear more conservative. Dark suits and ties for men and dresses or suits for women are always appropriate. Leave T-shirts, flip flops, jeans, fur, bold jewelry, and sneakers at home.

As for men, if you want to dress traditional, wear a white shirt. This includes a plain white shirt and a long, neutral necktie. However, there are always exceptions to the rules. A blue suit with a black turtleneck, black dress shirt with long red tie, black dress shirt (no tie, first button unbuttoned), or a black T-shirt (clean, kind of silky) could all be acceptable depending on the family. If you are a pall-bearer, you should expect to wear a suit or a dark sports coat and tie at the very least.

As for women, try to keep your dress simple but not too casual. Avoid "happy" patterns (i.e., flowers, martini glasses, or wild prints) or anything too flashy (i.e., sequins, unless minimal). Make sure that the only skin you display at a funeral is from the neck up and the knees down. A "sexy" dress, even if black, is not appropriate, as some churches prefer the shoulders remain covered.

Children should be appropriately dressed as well. Little boys should be outfitted in a black suit, possibly similar to their dad's suit. Little girls should wear a "box-like" dress, meaning it flows straight down from the shoulders, without any beading or sequins. For shoes, ballet flats may be a good choice for girls. Boys may wear black dress shoes or loafers (like dad's) or even plain black sneakers.

9.2 Memorial and Burial Service

9.2.1 Memorial Service

A *memorial service*, often called a funeral, is often officiated by a priest from the bereaved's church or religion, which may take place at either a funeral home or church. It is a service without the body present and can vary in ceremony and procedures according to the community and religious affiliations. It may be a very public event, attended by family, friends, colleagues, neighbors, and even acquaintances.

Those who were closest to the deceased may be asked to be a pall-bearer and carry the coffin. They will accompany the coffin to the altar and will also exit with the coffin. To do so is considered a great honor.

When seating yourself, please leave the first few rows empty for family members. Listen respectfully to those who are speaking. Any type of noise other than quiet whispering or mourning is considered disrespectful.

A Funeral Procession with Headlights on

Memorial services commonly include prayers, readings from a sacred text, hymns (sung either by the attendees or a hired vocalist), and words of comfort by the priest. Frequently, a relative or close friend will be asked to give a eulogy, which details happy memories and accomplishments. Often commenting on the deceased's flaws, especially at length, is considered impolite. Sometimes the delivering of the eulogy is done by the priest. Priests are often asked to deliver eulogies for the people they have never met. Church bells may also be tolled both before and after the service.

9.2.2 Burial Service

A *burial service* is conducted at the side of the grave, tomb, or cremation; at which the body of the deceased is buried or cremated at the conclusion. Sometimes, the burial service will immediately follow the funeral, in which case a funeral procession travels from the site of the memorial service to the burial site. Other times, the burial service takes place at a later time, when the final resting place is ready.

When driving in a funeral procession to the burial site, you're expected to drive in a slow, respectful manner with your headlights on. In a number of jurisdictions, special laws cover funeral processions—such as requiring other vehicles to give right-of-way to a funeral procession.

Some cultures consider it a sign of respect to deposit a ceremonial shovel of earth into the grave. This ceremony is initiated by a member of the family and followed by others. If you were close to the deceased, you may take your turn.

After the burial, it's common practice to go to the home of a family member or a restaurant for a reception. It is a symbol of the continuation of life and a moment of separation from the intense details of the death, funeral, and burial. This gives everyone a chance to talk and provides some time to relax and refresh.

9.3 Other Means to Express Sympathy

Besides paying a condolence visit and attending the funeral services as mentioned above, there are many other ways to express your sympathy.

Telephone calls. Speaking to a family member gives you an opportunity to offer your services and make them feel you really care. If they wish to discuss their recent loss, don't hesitate to talk to the person about the deceased. Be a good listener. Sending a telegram expressing your sympathy is also appropriate.

Flowers. Sending a floral tribute is a very appropriate way of expressing sympathy to the family of the deceased. Flowers express a feeling of life and beauty and offer much comfort to the family. It's customary to send flowers to the funeral home prior to the funeral or to the family residence at any time. If sent to the residence, usually a planter or a small vase of flowers indicating a person's continued sympathy for the family is suggested. An identification card is also placed on the floral tribute. At the funeral home the cards are removed from the floral tributes and given to the family so they may acknowledge the tributes sent.

Mass cards. Mass cards can be sent either by Catholic or non-Catholic friends. The offering of prayers is a valued expression of sympathy to a Catholic family. A card indicating that a Mass for the deceased has been arranged may be obtained from any Catholic parish. In some areas it is possible to obtain Mass cards at the funeral home. The Mass offering card or envelope is given to the family as an indication of understanding, faith, and compassion. Make sure that your name and address is legible and that you list your postal code. This will make it easier for the family to acknowledge your gift.

Sympathy cards. Sending a card of sympathy, even if you are only an acquaintance, is appropriate. It means so much to the family members to know they are in good thoughts. Depending on your relationship with the deceased, you can send a sympathy card instead or in addition to flowers, especially if you weren't able to attend the funeral. Make sure to send it as soon as possible.

Donations. Donations in memory of the deceased are often made, particularly when the family has requested donations in lieu of flowers. A donation may take various forms, including cash and other memorial gifts. The family is notified of the donations by personal note from the donor or through the donee, if the donee is a charity or other organization. In the latter case, the donor provides the family's name and address to the charity at the time the donation is made.

◆ Vocabulary ◆

condolence /kənˈdəʊləns/ ***n.*** an expression of sympathy with another's grief 吊唁

bereave /biˈriːv/ ***v.*** deprive through death (尤指死亡)使丧失(亲人、朋友等)

sympathy /ˈsimpəθi/ ***n.*** sharing the feelings of others (especially feelings of sorrow or anguish) 同情

clasp /klɑːsp/ ***v.*** hold firmly and tightly 握紧

overwhelm /ˌəʊvəˈwelm/ ***v.*** overpower in thought or feeling 使受不了

deceased /diˈsiːst/ ***a.*** dead 已故的 ***n.*** someone who is no longer alive 死者

visitation /ˌviziˈteiʃən/ ***n.*** a watch held over a corpse prior to burial 瞻仰遗体, 守灵

coffin /ˈkɔfin/ ***n.*** box in which a corpse is buried or cremated 棺材

meditate /ˌmediˈteit/ ***v.*** think intently and at length, as for spiritual purposes 冥想

eloquent /ˈeləkwənt/ ***a.*** expressing yourself readily, clearly, effectively 有说服力的

affiliation /əˌfiliˈeiʃən/ ***n.*** a social or business relationship 联系

descend /diˈsend/ ***v.*** come as if by falling 突然来临

subdued /səbˈdjuːd/ ***a.*** lacking in light; not bright or harsh 柔和的

hue /hjuː/ ***n.*** the quality of a color as determined by its dominant wavelength 色彩

grave /greiv/ ***n.*** a place for the burial of a corpse (especially beneath the ground and marked by a tombstone) 坟墓

flip flop /ˈflip ˌflɔp/ a rubber sandal loosely fastened to the foot by a thong 人字拖

bold /bəuld/ ***a.*** clear and distinct 醒目的

pall-bearer/ˈpɔːlbɛərə/ ***n.*** one of the mourners carrying the coffin at a funeral 抬棺人

martini /mɑːˈtiːni/ ***n.*** a cocktail made of gin (or vodka) with dry vermouth 马提尼酒

flashy /ˈflæʃi/ ***a.*** (used especially of clothes) marked by conspicuous display 浮华的

sequin /'si:kwin/ **n.** adornment consisting of a small piece of shiny material used to decorate (衣服上的圆形) 闪光装饰片

beading /'bi:diŋ/ **n.** ornamentation with beads 珠饰 (尤指花边状网眼边饰)

mourn /mɔ:n/ **v.** observe the customs of mourning after the death of a loved one 哀悼

sacred /'seikrid/ **a.** concerned with religion or religious purposes 宗教的, 神圣的

hymn /him/ **n.** a song of praise (to God or to a saint or to a nation) 赞美诗

vocalist /'vəukəlist/ **n.** a person who sings 歌手

eulogy /'ju:lədʒi/ **n.** a formal expression of praise 颂文

toll /təul/ **v.** ring slowly 缓慢敲响

tomb /tu:m/ **n.** a grave, especially a large one (尤指较大的) 坟墓

cremation /kri'meiʃən/ **n.** the incineration of a dead body 火葬

headlight /'hed,lait/ **n.** a powerful light with reflector usually attached to the front of an automobile or locomotive (汽车等的) 前灯

jurisdiction /dʒuəris'dikʃən/ **n.** in law; the territory within which power can be exercised 司法辖区

deposit /di'pɔzit/ **v.** put something down 放置

shovel /'ʃʌvl/ **n.** a hand tool for lifting loose material; consists of a curved container or scoop and a handle 铲子

floral /'flɔ:rəl/ **a.** relating to or associated with flowers 用花装饰的

tribute /'tribju:t/ **n.** something given or contributed voluntarily as due or deserved; especially a gift showing respect, gratitude or affection 敬献的礼物

Mass card (Roman Catholic Church) a card sent to a bereaved family that says the sender has arranged for a Mass to be said in memory of the deceased 弥撒卡片

parish /'pæriʃ/ **n.** a local church community 教区

compassion /kəm'pæʃən/ **n.** a deep awareness of and sympathy for another's suffering 怜悯, 同情

legible /'ledʒəbəl/ **a.** (of handwriting, print, etc.) able to be read 清晰可辨的

donation /dəu'neiʃən/ **n.** a voluntary gift (as of money or service) made to some worthwhile cause 捐赠物

in lieu of instead of 代替

charity /'tʃæriti/ **n.** an institution set up to provide help to the needy 慈善机构

◆ Exercises ◆

I. Translation

Directions: *In this part there are 10 words or phrases in English. Please translate them into Chinese.*

1. condolence visit   2. funeral home   3. pall-bearer

4. coffin   5. eulogy   6. the deceased

7. memorial service   8. burial service   9. floral tribute

10. sympathy card

II. Blank filling

Directions: *In this part there is one passage with several incomplete sentences. Please fill in all the blanks.*

In many cultures, the first event that follows a death is _____, also referred to as a calling or wake. It is typically held at the _____ within a few days before the actual funeral memorial service. Visitation provides a time and place for friends to offer their expression of sorrow and sympathy.

If you attend a visitation you should approach the family and express your _____. As with the condolence visit it is appropriate to relate your memories of the _____. It is customary to show your respects by viewing the deceased if the body is present and the _____ is open. You may wish to say a silent _____ for, or meditate about, the deceased at this time. Normally your _____ name should be listed on the register book.

III. Essay questions

Directions: *In this part there are two essay questions. Please write the corresponding answer for each question.*

1. Suppose when you are studying abroad, you hear of the death of one of your classmates due to a car accident. He was your good friend and came from a Catholic family. His parents also know you well. Upon receiving the bad news, what would you do?

2. What are the differences between memorial service and burial service? What are the dress codes for those occasions?

Situational Dialogues

Dialogue 1

(A condolence visit)

Helen: Alice, I'm deeply sorry to hear about your grandmother. She was a wonderful person, and I loved her like my own grandmother.

Alice: Thank you for your sympathy. I'm deeply touched. She loved you, too.

Helen: Please let me know if there's anything I can do. I brought over some fried chicken. I know you have enough things to worry about without having to think about cooking.

Alice: That was really thoughtful, Helen. And thanks for the flowers, too. They're beautiful.

Helen: Well, I'll let you go now. There are a lot of other people waiting to talk to you, and I'll see you tomorrow. In the meantime, if there's anything at all I can do, don't hesitate to ask me.

Alice: Thanks, Helen. I will.

海伦：爱丽丝，听到你祖母不幸的消息，我感到非常难过。她是个非常好的人，我爱她就像爱自己的祖母一样。

爱丽丝：谢谢你的好心。我非常感动，她也非常爱你。

海伦：如果需要帮助，请告诉我。我带了一只炸鸡，我知道你烦心的事太多就不会想着做饭。

爱丽丝：你真体贴人，海伦。也谢谢你的花，它们很漂亮。

海伦：你去照顾别人吧，有许多人在等着和你谈话。我明天再来看你。还有，如果有需要帮忙的地方尽管找我。

爱丽丝：谢谢海伦，我会的。

Dialogue 2

(Viewing the deceased)

Jin: I don't know what to say. This can't be happening. Here's the obituary.

Sarah: It's really there? It's all one big nightmare.

Jin: But it explains why Tom isn't answering the phone and Fanny took time off from work.

Sarah: Poor Fanny. Tom's death must have made her realize that she still cared for him.

Jin: This says the viewing is at Myers Funeral Home today until five.

Sarah: It's already half past four. We should go and pay our respects. Tom's family will be there.

Jin: Don't we need to give a white envelope with money for the family, though?

Sarah: No. People give plates of food. The food is brought to the reception or in the weeks following.

Jin: At the reception?

Sarah: That's after the funeral. That way the family doesn't need to think about cooking while they are mourning.

Jin: What else can be brought besides food?

Sarah: You can bring flowers if you want.

金：我不知道该说什么。这不可能发生。这儿有讣告。

莎拉：真的有？这真是一场噩梦。

金：但这解释了汤姆为什么不接电话，范妮请假没去上班。

莎拉：可怜的范妮。汤姆的死肯定让她意识到自己仍那么在乎他。

金：讣告上说遗体瞻仰在梅叶思殡仪馆，到五点结束。

莎拉：现在都四点半了。我们应该去向汤姆告别。汤姆的家人也会在那儿的。

金：我们不需要带点钱装在白色信封里给他家里人送过去吗？

莎拉：不需要。人们一般只带食物。在丧宴上或在随后的几个星期内带食物过去。

金：丧宴？

莎拉：那是在葬礼之后。这样逝者的家属就不需要在悼念期间还要考虑做饭的事情了。

金：除了食物还可以带点什么？

莎拉：如果你想的话可以带花去。

Supplementary Reading

中国丧葬礼仪

Funeral Story

By Charles Baron

This is a true story of an experience I just had. Only the names are changed.

Last Thursday at 6 p.m., I got a call from a woman who said she was looking for someone to conduct a Humanistic funeral for her uncle, a North Miami Beach man who died Tuesday at the age of 89. I said I could probably do it, when will it be? "Tomorrow at 3:00," she said.

Sarah explained that she lived in Queens, she was his only close living relative, and she had been making many calls to find someone to do a Humanist ceremony. Her Uncle Max, 7 years ago, gave her the name and number of a Humanist guy he desired to conduct his future funeral ceremony. The number was no longer good, and the guy was nowhere to be found. She found Humanist literature in her uncle's apartment. and called the AHA (American Humanist Assoc.), and they referred her to the Humanists of Fla. Assoc., whose president (in Tampa) referred her to me.

Although I had plans for office paper pushing the next day, I had no Friday. Afternoon appointments, and the ceremony was to be at a funeral home right down the street from my office, so I said, "OK, let's meet tonight." I met her at the uncle's apartment. At one of those complexes (建筑群) with a zillion (庞大的数字) one-bedroom apartments on catwalks. "Tell me about your uncle," I said. She explained that although she herself is a believer and attends a Conservative Shul (but doesn't keep kosher because she loves Chinese food and shrimp), her uncle was a very strict atheist, so she wanted to honor his wishes, his way of thinking.

Max had a life with a lot of hard times. Raised in Brooklyn by Greek Jewish parents, he lost his father at the age of 17 and had to help raise his three younger siblings (兄弟姐妹). For that reason, he never wanted kids of his own. He fought in World War Ⅱ, experiencing the horrors of war. Never married, he was a printer by trade and once had a radio shop. He retired to Florida 20 years ago for the weather and the less expensive lifestyle.

17 years ago, his sister (Sarah's mom) died, and ever since then he and Sarah spoke on the phone every Sunday morning. Sarah and her husband and kids would sometimes also come down and visit—but they could NEVER move to Florida because everyone is just so slow here, like the grocery cashier chatting with the customer in front of her the other day when all she wanted was to get a bottle of water and get out of there! On top of that, "We are liberal New Yorkers, and your politics here are yuck (令人反感的事物). We couldn't imagine living in a place that elects a Jeb

Bush."

Max was a scientific thinker, liked to tinker (摆弄) with radio equipment and fix things. Sarah and Max got into phone discussions over the years about God, and he would say that without scientific proof of a supernatural being, he was unable to believe.

They grew close, and he gave Sarah a lot of money over the years. One year, they got into a yelling match on the phone because he was upset that she sent her two daughters to religious school, so he felt she was misusing his gift money. She finally told him, "If you want to have a say about raising kids, go have your own!"—and has felt bad about that ever since.

Max became an avid (热心的) ballroom dancer at a local dancing club, a favorite activity. A girlfriend followed him down from New York, but he wanted to "play the field," so didn't stay steady with her. Then the girlfriend died in a car accident 10 years ago, and he was devastated (摧毁).

Sarah will spread his ashes at Brighton Beach, New York, where Max "loved to hang out with his cronies (伙伴)."

So that was the story from this lady who called me out of the blue to do a funeral. I told her about our group, which she never heard of. (She didn't know she would find a Jewish Humanist—she was looking for any Humanist.) There's also a Humanistic Jewish group in Queens, I told her. That rang a bell—"now that you mention it, I do remember seeing ads for them," she said.

I read her a small sample of our funeral readings. "Fine," she said, while the look on her face was like, "that's kind of odd."

Since dancing was the biggest joy of Max's life, I looked through the readings for something that would apply, in vain. Then I flipped (快速翻动) through a few issues of Jewish Currents, which has all kinds of poems, and found this right before showtime:

On My Eightieth Birthday

(by Muriel Harris Weinstein)

I want a flowery dress of slinky silk,

bursting with tropical blossoms

where purple and fuschia hibiscus cascade over breasts

in such abundance everyone will say,

"Ahh, the Hanging Gardens of Babylon."

I want young vines to entwine my waist

and slide over my hips in green ecstasy,

ribbon out with each hip's sway,

shimmy with each thigh's thrust.

I want to strut past the Senior Center

where guys will throw down their canes
and walkers and bump into each other
rushing to my side...to inhale my floral fragrance.

I want tiger lilies, oleander, bougainvillaea
and orchids, to grow along the hem
bloom in collision of chaotic colors
and my feet will dance in that garden

The ruffles on my skirt bounce and flirt,
swing around my legs to jazz I'm improvising
and my song will grow crescendoing
past tongue and lips
as I swing my hips and sing
till I reach the end.

I threw it in my briefcase, and in a black suit and cheerful tie, headed to the funeral home. I greeted the funeral home director and explained I'm from the Secular Jewish Humanists and would be doing a cultural, non-theistic ceremony. He asked me what cue would signal the ceremony is about to end; it'll be a moment of silence, I said. As I passed the yarmulke (圆顶小帽) stand without taking one, I saw a U.S. flag folded in a triangular clear plastic case lying on the casket to honor Max the Vet.

Attending besides Sarah were about ten friends of Max's, consisting of women from the dance club, plus his home health aide (助手) and the owner of a Hallandale thrift shop where Max liked to go and fix things for free. The casket was opened, they said "goodbye," and a woman made the sign of the cross on her chest as it was closed again.

We got started, and I explained that this would be a Humanist ceremony, honoring Max who was a Humanist, believing in ethics, rationality, and dignity, but not religious. I hit the highlights of his life, did some readings and then the poem, which they liked. There were informal, spontaneous (自发的) eulogies. The thrift shop guy said, "God bless him—I know he didn't believe that, but I'll miss him and God bless him!" I concluded with the moment of silence and some final words. The funeral home guy came in, took the flag and solemnly stated to Sarah as she was in tears, "On behalf of the United States of America, I present to you this flag."

I thanked everyone for coming and mentioned I am an attorney and this is a hobby. A dance lady said, "I can't stand my attorney—give me your card, you seem easy to get along with." Then everyone else asked for a card, too. I handed them out, right there in front of the casket, then thought to myself it would have been better to ask them to come into the next room. Next time.

Chapter 10
Business Etiquette

商务礼仪

在本章中，你将了解到：
- 商务会晤的礼仪
- 商务会餐和赠礼应注意些什么
- 正式商务会议的礼仪
- 办公室礼仪
- 面试礼仪

Intensive Reading

10.1 Business Visiting

10.1.1 Making Appointments

Making a business appointment is the first step in selling your business' products or services. Prior appointments for meetings are necessary. Appointments should be made at least a few days in advance, and ideally, confirmed on arrival. Most businessmen in Western countries tend to decline to meet a visitor even on a relatively short notice.

It's best to avoid making business appointments around the dates of public holidays. For instance, July and August might be the months when those with children are almost obliged to take their annual summer vacation. National days and the days between Christmas and New Year should certainly be avoided. Easter is also popular for holidays in most Western countries. In the United Kingdom and Ireland, there are two Bank Holidays in May that may catch the unwary visitors while in the United States and Canada, Thanksgiving Day is a grand festival similar to Christmas Day.

Propose a time and let the customer come back with an alternative if they wish. That way you remain in control rather than giving the customer an obvious chance to stall. It's best to arrange appointments mid-morning and mid-afternoon. Breakfast meetings are rare and it is also unlikely to arrange an initial meeting involving lunch or dinner.

Punctuality in some countries, such as Austria and Germany, is renowned throughout the world. Make every effort to arrive for a meeting at the appointed time. Never arrive late and arrive no more than five minutes early. On the other hand, you can be fashionably late for *social events*. You are allowed to arrive a respectable 15 minutes after the specific time. For instance, if a dinner invitation states "7:30 p.m. to 8:00 p.m.," it means you will be expected at about 7:50 p.m.

If you cannot make your scheduled appointment time, call as soon as you know. If you are running late for your appointment, please call the customer as soon as you know that you are going to be late. Do not wait until the time of your scheduled appointment to call and say you're still 15 or 20 minutes away or you can't make it.

10.1.2 Business Attire

Having an elegant work get-up is important. It encourages others to take you seriously. Your business attire should be as professional as possible no matter what your age is.

As for men, business suit and tie are always appropriate. Wear dark colored business suits in classic colors of gray and navy. For an important formal meeting, choose a white dress shirt. For a less formal meeting, a light blue shirt will still give you a conservative appearance. Keep your business clothes clean and well pressed. Also remember to keep your shoes clean. Dirty shoes can throw off your seemingly polished appearance.

Women should wear a suit or dress with jacket. Wearing classic clothing and classic colors of navy, gray, ivory, and white will ensure you give a confident and conservative appearance. Keep your hemline conservative, about one or two inches above the knee. This length is not only more attractive but suitable for most women.

Dress codes vary from company to company and among positions even within companies, as different working environments demand different styles of attire. Follow the dress code if you receive an invitation. When in doubt, always overdress for circumstances.

When attending business functions, keep business cards in your pocket for easy access. Besides, do not overfill your briefcase or handbag for it will create a disorganized look.

10.1.3 Communications

Business Telephone Etiquette. The telephone has become an indispensable tool in businesses today. It is imperative to know all the rules while talking on a phone for business purposes. Good telephone etiquettes will leave a good impression of your organization on both the callers and the called.

If you are in a company that takes quite a bit of incoming calls, answer with the company's name first and greet the person depending on the time of the day, e.g., "Bloomingdale's, Good morning!" While calling you should introduce yourself and give the name of your organization if you are working in one, e.g., "This is Mary Kate from Star Electronics. May I speak to Nicole Richie please?"

You should always conduct yourself in a professional businesslike manner. Speak clearly and slowly when taking a business call. You should not mumble and never eat food or chew gum while talking on the phone. Keep phone calls brief and friendly. Try to call during the day as much as possible. Calls before 9 am and after 9 pm should be avoided.

Business Greetings. Greet everyone with a firm and sincere handshake, a friendly smile, and direct eye contact upon arrival and departure. When approaching a group of individuals, it's important to note that guests should always shake the hand of the host first.

Business cards are generally exchanged at the beginning of or at the end of an initial meeting. Good business etiquette requires you to present the card so the recipient's language is face up.

When receiving any business card, make a point of studying it, commenting on it, and clarifying information before putting it away.

As for business introductions, there are two basic rules: (i) Introduce lower ranking individuals to higher ranking individuals. (ii) Remember to include titles (e.g., Dr., Judge, etc.,) or name prefix (e.g., Mr., Mrs., Ms.) and the full name. If you forget someone's name, you can sometimes "cover" by introducing a person you do know first. For example using, "Do you know Joe Smith, one of our account reps?" will usually get the unknown person to introduce him or herself. If this doesn't work, an admission that you've had a mental block is preferable.

10.2 Business Meals and Gift Giving

10.2.1 Business Meals

Doing business over meals is a ritual that has existed for centuries. Taking clients to breakfast, lunch, or dinner has long been an effective way to build relationships, make the sale, or seal the deal. Since breakfast meetings are rare, we'll focus on business lunches and dinners.

Plan ahead when you issue the invitation. Allow a week for a business dinner and three days for lunch (things like selecting a restaurant, making your reservation, etc.). Send a reminder email to confirm the meal appointment with your clients a day before the meeting.

Upon the meeting, arrive early so you can attend to last minute details. Take charge of the seating. Your guests should have the prime seats—the ones with the view. As the host, take the least desirable spot—the one facing the wall, the kitchen or the restrooms.

When your client arrives, offering a handshake and greeting with a good afternoon is proper etiquette. Saying something like "Thank you for taking your precious time for this meeting" will be good. If there is a large group from a single firm, meet the senior most with regards to the position and then accordingly the others. Please do not forget to switch off or put your cell phone on silent mode. This is a very crucial aspect of business lunch or dinner etiquette.

Just to give the conversation a kick start, small talk is required. Break it when the waiter comes for your order. Allow your guest to order first. If your food does not come before the client's, ask the client to go ahead with his, lest it gets cold. Slowly get into the business mode. As the host, you are the one who decides when to start discussing business. That will depend on a number of factors such as the time of day and how well you know your clients. At lunch, wait until you have ordered so you won't be interrupted. At dinner, the more social occasion, limit the business talk and do it after the main course is completed. Limit the amount of alcohol you drink at the business meal. If the customer has wine it is okay for you to have a little wine. But remember being in high spirits at such a meeting is a huge no-no in business meal etiquette.

When it comes to the problem area about who pays, it has to be you, obviously! To make this affair discreet, there are many ways. To start off, before you take your place, ask the waiter to give you the bill directly. The client or your guest should not even know ideally that you paid the bill.

What you can also do is, as and when you are sure that you are not going to order anything more, excuse yourself and pay at the reception directly. This will avoid any ambiguity as to who will pay.

Finally, give a good enough tip and walk the guest out and ensure that he is comfortably on his way. You should never leave before the client. Last but not least, it is a good idea to send a follow up thank-you note to the guest. Even in case you haven't been able to strike a deal. It could be a physical note or an email for his graciousness of having given you time, which leaves a positive impression.

10.2.2 Gift Giving

In general gifts are given in business to promote goodwill and foster good relationships. They are also given to show appreciation.

First, if you are dealing in international trade you should make yourself knowledgeable about the customs of those you would like to gift. For instance, a leather pencil holder would be a fine gift in the US, but a major faux pas in India, where cows are sacred.

Another big consideration is to give a gift that you know the recipient will appreciate. Do a little research; find out what their interests and hobbies are. They will be very impressed that you took the time to discover what they like and will feel comfortable in knowing that this wasn't just some anonymous purchase.

Just keep in mind what the perceived value is in the culture of the person you are gifting. For example a person from Mexico would think lowly of a gift of silver because it is cheap and abundant there. Chocolate is a gift that can have two different perceptions. If you give someone chocolate that came from Wal-Mart they may perceive that as cheap, but if you give them expensive imported French chocolate they will consider that thoughtful. Remember it all depends on the person. Gifts should be for a specific individual based upon what you know or have learned about them.

Gifts need not (and generally should not) be expensive. Make the gift modest and not appear to be a bribe. The amount of the gift depends upon the hierarchy in the company. The higher position a person holds the more expensive the gift should be. Also, be sure to never give similar gifts to all those you are gifting.

If you select to feature your corporate logo on the gift, be sure the item is useful and of the highest quality, with the logo discreetly imprinted. This gift will serve as a permanent reminder of your organization, and the recipient will likely use it if the logo is understated.

The presentation of the gift is almost as important as the value of the present itself. The packaging enhances the item's perception of value. The box should be of good quality, elegantly wrapped with a card enclosed, and presented in person, if possible.

10.3 Formal Business Meetings

Formal meetings can take many forms. There are board meetings, management meetings, team or departmental meetings, and business negotiations. While meetings may differ in terms of their content, they'll usually have a similar structure overall. For instance, a chairperson, minutes to attend to, a set-out agenda. The etiquette is almost the same for each formal meeting, something that everyone is aware of.

Punctuality is a crucial factor when it comes to formal meetings. In fact, you should not be on time, you should be present at the spot at least five minutes beforehand. Being late is not only considered rude but also reflects the nature of the person. If you do reach late due to some reason, go and sit in your place without disturbing the proceedings. If you are organizing the meeting, start it on time, irrespective of the attendance. Do not make the present members wait only because some members are late.

You should dress appropriately for the meeting. It has to be formal attire. Dress like a professional. T-shirts and jeans are out of question when it comes to a meeting. There won't be any dress code mentioned, however, you are expected to dress in clean and neat clothes; also pay attention to your footwear. Make sure that your socks are not torn or have any holes, and polish the shoes before the meeting.

Talking about manners, keep your cell phone switched off during the meeting. If it is not possible to switch it off, keep it on silent in your pocket, on silent. Do not keep it on the table as the vibration will disturb the meeting.

If you're unsure about where to sit, ask—don't just sit down anywhere. The person leading the meeting sits at the head of the table, usually opposite the entry door so he or she can see people coming in. If a key customer is attending the meeting, that power seat would be reserved for him or her. The second most important position is to the power position's right, the third to his/her left. The most competitive seat in relation to the power seat is directly across. All of this applies to traditional board-room-type seating, such as long rectangular tables. But positioning also applies to meetings at round tables. The only difference is where the boss sits, and then everyone else tends to sit in the above-noted places in relation to the meeting leader.

Preparation is important. If you are given references to the meeting beforehand, take the trouble to familiarize yourself with all this paperwork prior to the meeting. Do not waste your and others people's time beating around the bush. Speak only about the concerned topic, in short and simple sentences. Do not go on talking as there are also other people who wish to talk, be precise and wrap your presentation within a certain time. Be prepared for questions that might be asked about the topic. If you cannot answer a certain query, honestly tell the person asking. Do not give vague or rude answers. Also carry a pen, pencil, notepad, laptop, etc., with you.

Listening attentively is also an important etiquette. You shouldn't interrupt mid-speech even if you don't agree with something. What you should do is to take a note of the issue and come back to that later when it's your turn to speak, if appropriate. Keep eye contact 80%—90% of the time.

10.4 Office Etiquette

Following etiquettes at a workplace is very important. It is generally the key deciding factor in how your colleagues will respond to you and come to your rescue when you require help. Further, the way one conducts themselves in the office with people who eventually become a part of a second family speaks a lot about the kind of person that one is.

There are a number of things that you should do if you want to be seen as a valuable member of the team and to be considered a valued colleague. These can include:

- Discover how things are done by your colleagues and why. Conform to an office's working model.

- Be acquainted with people from all rungs of the ladder, from the boss to the post room.

- Be respectful and courteous towards others—even if you don't necessarily like a particular person.

- Keep your voice at an acceptable level. A loud voice which is noticeable in a particular work environment can not only be counterproductive for others who are trying to get on with their work but can be extremely annoying too.

- Offer to help others if there's anything you might be able to do to assist them and make their job easier if you've time to do so.

- Make sure you understand the rules surrounding E-mail etiquette and the use of your mobile phone.

- Remember you're being paid to work so keep idle chit-chat and other things that may take your attention away from what you've been employed to do to a minimum.

- Keep your work area tidy. Try not to be messy.

- Stay positive and upbeat and...smile!

Often, it's a simple matter of using your common sense and behaving in a manner that shows courtesy and respect for others but there are numerous things that you should obviously not get involved with or encourage. Here's a list of some of the most commonly cited examples of behavior that is often frowned upon and not even tolerated by most companies, regardless of type. Disregarding these, it can often, at best, make you unpopular or, at worst, might even get you the sack. Things you shouldn't do at work include:

- Never discuss salary with your colleagues.

- Don't engage in idle gossip about other colleagues or your boss or 'bad mouth' them. Gossips are usually presumed to be untrustworthy.

- Don't get involved in any jokes which might have sexual or racial overtones.

- Be modest and don't harp on about any of your previous achievements or be an attention seeker.

- Don't try to court favor with your boss or immediate supervisors. Just doing your job in the best way you can is the most productive way of impressing those higher up the ladder than you.

● Don't assume something is acceptable practice in either conversations you might have or actions you might consider taking. A good example of this is assuming that it's OK to leave your mobile phone on silent or vibrate, yet still respond to text messages. Establish the position on that and other things you're not sure about first such as eating at your desk or work station, which is another good example where people often do the wrong thing.

10.5 Job Interview Etiquette

10.5.1 Dressing Accordingly

At an interview, proper etiquette dictates that your manner of dress should by and large fit in with the scene around you. In a show of respect for the occasion, you should dress just a step above the norm of that environment. The reason is because inappropriate business attire—in either direction, up or down—creates an unacceptable distraction. When the focus should be on you and all your skills, your clothes shouldn't be stealing the show.

Consider these examples, in which a pattern is clearly visible: If everyone at the workplace wears jeans and T-shirts, wear slacks and a long-sleeved button-down shirt. If they're in slacks and button-down shirts, wear a coat and consider a tie.

10.5.2 Be Punctual

One of the biggest etiquette mistakes a job-seeker can make is arriving late. Arrive at least 15-30 minutes early to the job interview. Whether you're simply going across town or driving a great distance, always know the route you're going to take; take a practice run (if possible); and factor in extra time for getting lost, street closures, and accidents. Finally, don't overstay your welcome—even if your return flight is hours away. When the interviews are done, say your thank-you and leave.

10.5.3 Be Polite

Showcase your inner strengths by patiently waiting your turn to speak with recruiters or hiring managers, properly shake hands (dry, firm, one-handed shake), and address the each person by his or her title (Dr., Ms., Mr.) and last name. Sit when invited to do so. There are times in job-hunting in which assertiveness is important (to demonstrate your interest in the job), but there is no excuse for not being polite.

10.5.4 Present a Positive Personal Image

Even if you are having a bad day, do not let outside circumstances affect your manner in a job-search situation. A positive attitude—which includes things like enthusiasm, smiling, good posture, and strong eye contact—can go a long way to making a lasting and positive impression. People want to work with happy and friendly people.

10.5.5 Three Definite DON'TS:

DON'T get caught unprepared. Learning as much as you can about the company and about the position for which you're applying is a sign of respect. As simple as it sounds, don't forget that your interviewer works for this company; it's a big part of this person's life. Therefore, a modest but competent display of your commitment to this interview through prior research makes you look good while flattering them at the same time.

DON'T disparage past employers. If you can't say something nice about someone, don't say anything. It's disrespectful to take shots at former employers and companies (in part because they're not around to defend themselves), and doing so can seem cheap and offensive to others. Furthermore, the interview is about you and this company and how you fit together. Don't leave your interviewer with descriptions of former bosses and coworkers who have nothing to do with the job interview.

DON'T lie—about anything. For all the many reasons not to lie or to wildly embellish anything, remember that a gentleman never lies. He doesn't need to. Neither does a lady.

10.5.6 Thank Them "Twice"

At the end of the interview, when you will invariably thank your interviewer, make sure to thank them both for their time as well as for your own opportunity. Much like arriving on time, thanking them in this way sends a message that you understand and appreciate the value of one's time.

Don't consider the interview completely over until, that evening, you have written a short thank-you note. Keep it short. E-mail is acceptable but snail mail is preferred. Since this is a business communication, it shouldn't be handwritten.

◆ Vocabulary ◆

obliged /əˈblaidʒd/ **a.** under a moral obligation to do something 有义务的，有必要的

unwary /ʌnˈwɛəri/ *a.* not alert to danger or deception 不注意的，粗心的

get-up /ˈgetʌp/ *n.* outfit, costume 装束，打扮

function /ˈfʌŋkʃən/ *n.* a formal or official social gathering or ceremony 重要集会

indispensable /ˌindisˈpensəbl/ *a.* absolutely necessary 必不可少的

imperative /imˈperətiv/ *a.* not to be avoided, necessary 必要的

mumble /ˈmʌmbl/ *v.* talk indistinctly; usually in a low voice 含糊地说，咕哝

rep /rep/ *n.* informal abbreviation of "representative" 销售代表

ritual /ˈritʃuəl/ *n.* any customary observance or practice 惯例

seal /siːl/ *v.* decide irrevocably 确定，使成定局

discreet /disˈkriːt/ *a.* marked by prudence or modesty and wise self-restraint 谨慎的

ambiguity /ˌæmbiˈgjuːiti/ *n.* unclearness by virtue of having more than one meaning 模棱两可的意思

faux pas /ˈfəu ˈpɑː/ *n.* a socially awkward or tactless act 失礼

anonymous /əˈnɔniməs/ *a.* not known or lacking marked individuality 没特色的

bribe /braib/ *n.* payment made to a person in a position of trust to corrupt his judgment 贿赂

imprint /imˈprint/ *v.* mark or stamp with or as if with pressure 印上，压印

understate /ˌʌndəˈsteit/ *v.* represent as less significant or important 很有节制地陈述或表达 (某事物)

minutes /ˈminits/ *n.* a written account of what transpired at a meeting 会议记录

agenda /əˈdʒendə/ *n.* a list of matters to be taken up (as at a meeting) 议程表

irrespective /ˌirisˈpektiv/ *a.* in spite of everything; without regard to drawbacks 不顾的，与……无关的

familiarize /fəˈmiljəˌraiz/ *v.* make familiar or acquainted 使熟悉

query /ˈkwiəri/ *n.* an instance of questioning 问题，询问

rung /rʌŋ/ *n.* one of the crosspieces that form the steps of a ladder 阶梯

counterproductive /ˈkauntəprəˌdʌktiv/ *a.* tending to hinder the achievement of a goal 使达不到预期目标的

chit-chat /ˈtʃit-ˌtʃæt/ *n.* small talk, gossip 闲聊，叽叽喳喳

upbeat /ˈʌpbiːt/ *a.* pleasantly (even unrealistically) optimistic 积极向上的

untrustworthy /ʌnˈtrʌstwəːθi/ *a.* not worthy of trust or belief 不能信赖的

overtone /ˈəuvəˌtəun/ *n.* (usually plural) an ulterior implicit meaning or quality 暗示，含义

harp /hɑːp/ *v.* come back to 唠叨，喋喋不休地说

court /kɔːt/ *v.* make amorous advances towards 讨好，奉承

supervisor /ˈsjuːpəˌvaizə/ *n.* one who supervises or has charge and direction of 主管

closure /ˈkləuʒə/ *n.* the act of blocking (路或桥的) 暂时封闭

showcase /ˈʃəuˌkeis/ *v.* to exhibit esp. in an attractive or favorable aspect 使展示(优点) *n.* a setting in which something can be displayed to best effect 展示(本领、才华或优良品质)的场合

assertiveness /əˈsəːtivnis/ *n.* bold self-confidence 过分自信

disparage /dɪˈspærɪdʒ/ *v.* express a negative opinion of 贬低

embellish /emˈbelɪʃ/ *v.* make more attractive by adding ornament, color, etc.美化，修饰

◆ **Exercises** ◆

Ⅰ. Translation

Directions: *In this part there are 10 words or phrases in English. Please translate them into Chinese.*

1. National Day　　　　2. punctuality　　　　3. business card

4. client　　　　　　　5. small talk　　　　6. corporate logo

7. chairperson　　　　8. set-out agenda　　9. recruiter

10. job-hunting

Ⅱ. Blank filling

Directions: *In this part there is one short passage with several incomplete sentences. Please fill in all the blanks.*

When attending a business meeting, don't just sit down anywhere. If you are not sure where to sit, don't hesitate to ask.

The person leading the meeting sits at the _____ of the table, usually opposite the entry door so he or she can see people coming in. This is called the _____. If a _____ is attending the meeting, that power seat should be reserved for him or her. The second most important position is to the power position's _____, the third to his/her _____. The most competitive seat in relation to the power seat is directly _____. All of this applies to traditional board-room-type seating, such as long _____ tables. Positioning also applies to meetings at round tables. The only difference is where the boss sits, and then everyone else tends to sit in the above-noted places in relation to the meeting leader.

Ⅲ. Essay questions

Directions: *In this part there are two essay questions. Please write the corresponding answer for each question.*

1. Suppose your boss puts the responsibility of cracking a deal at a luncheon business meeting with

a potential client on you. How will you contact the client and arrange this business lunch? List key points.

2．If you get the chance of an interview from the company you really want to come aboard, how will you plan and behave at the job interview? Write a resume of your own.

Situational Dialogues

Dialogue 1

(Help for job hunting)

Kirchner: Hi, Liz, take a seat. What can I do for you?

Liz: Thank you. I'm graduating, and I need a resume to apply for a job with a foreign company. Could you tell me how to write a resume?

Kirchner: Sure. First your resume should start with your name, sex, age, address and telephone number. Second, you should include the education you have received, experience you have, and foreign languages you have studied.

Liz: Is that all?

Kirchner: No, you may also put in your hobbies and any other personal factors. They might be useful, too. Besides which, you should also include the major job objective you have in mind.

Liz: Thank you very much, Professor Kirchner. See you tomorrow.

Kirchner: See you.

(The next day, Liz has prepared her resume, and she is talking to Professor Kirchner about it.)

Liz: Good morning, Professor Kirchner. I have written my resume. Could you go over it and see if I need to make any changes?

Kirchner: Certainly. You have studied for two years in this university, attended No. 1 Middle School in Jilin and had some work experience as well.

Liz: Yes, I have worked as the chairperson of the Student Union since I came to the university and I had a part-time job as managing assistant during my vacations.

Kirchner: From your resume, I can see you are good at both English and German. I believe you're likely to get what you want: An assistant manager's position.

Liz: Thanks for your encouragement. So my resume is all right?

Kirchner: Sure. Good luck, Liz!

Liz: Thank you, bye!

柯克纳：你好，莉兹，请坐。我能帮你做点什么？

莉兹：谢谢您。我就要毕业了，我需要写一份个人简历，到一家外企求职。请问应该怎样写简历？

柯克纳：好的，你的简历应从姓名、性别、年龄、住址及电话开始。其次，你还要写上你所受的教育，你的工作经历，以及你学的外语。

莉兹：就这么多么？

柯克纳：不，你还可以写上你的爱好和其他的个人情况，这些都会有用。此外，你还应把所希望的主要求职目标加上去。

莉兹：非常感谢，柯克纳教授。明天见。

柯克纳：再见。

(第二天，莉兹写好了简历，正与柯克纳教授商讨。)

莉兹：柯克纳教授，早上好。我的简历写完了。您能帮我看一下需要做些什么改动吗？

柯克纳：当然可以。你在这所大学读了两年，中学就读于吉林第一中学，还有一些工作经历。

莉兹：是的，自从上大学以来，我一直担任学生会主席。另外，假期我还兼职干过经理助理的工作。

柯克纳：以你的简历来看，你还精通英语和德语。我觉得你能够得到你想要的经理助理的职务。

莉兹：谢谢您的鼓励。这么说我的简历可以了？

柯克纳：当然。莉兹，祝你好运。

莉兹：谢谢您，再见！

Dialogue 2

(Meeting a guest)

Zhang: Excuse me, aren't you Mr. Thompson from New Jersey?

Thompson: Yes. And you are...

Zhang: I'm Zhang Lin from Zhejiang Import and Export Company.

Thompson: How do you do, Mr. Zhang? Thanks for meeting me at the airport.

Zhang: You're welcome. I'm very pleased to meet you.

Thompson: Do you know where the baggage claim area is?

Zhang: Yes, it's over there. How many pieces of luggage do you have?

Thompson: Only one suitcase.

Zhang: Let's go.

Thompson: OK.

Zhang: How's your flight?

西 方 社 会 礼 仪 与 文 化

Thompson: Just wonderful! Good food and good service.

Zhang: Is it your first time to Hangzhou?

Thompson: Yes. I hope it won't be my last.

Zhang: Next time you come, please bring your wife along.

Thompson: I will.

Zhang: Face to face contact is good for both sides.

Thompson: Yes. That's why I am here.

Zhang: By the way, how's business these days?

Thompson: Not bad. But sales are down a bit due to inflation.

Zhang: Do you think it's just a lasting trend?

Thompson: Oh, I hope not. I think it's just a slump.

Zhang: I hope so.

Thompson: Look, that's my suitcase.

Zhang: Our car is out in the parking lot. We'll take you to the hotel.

Thompson: Very good.

张：对不起，你是不是新泽西来的汤普森先生？

汤普森：不错，你是……

张：我是浙江进出口公司的张林。

汤普森：你好，张先生。谢谢你来机场接我。

张：别客气，很高兴来接你。

汤普森：你知道行李认领处在哪儿吗？

张：知道，就在那边。你带了几件行李？

汤普森：就一个行李包。

张：走吧。

汤普森：好的。

张：旅程怎么样？

汤普森：棒极了！可口的食物，优质的服务。

张：这是你第一次来杭州吗？

汤普森：不错。但愿这不是最后一次。

张：下次来的时候，请携贵夫人一起来。

汤普森：我会的。

张：当面会晤对双方都有利。

汤普森：是的，这也是我来的缘由。

张：顺便问一下，最近业务如何？

汤普森：还不错。不过由于货币升值销量略有下降。

张：你认为这是总体趋势吗？

汤普森：噢，希望并非如此。我想只不过是一次暴跌，情况会好转的。

张：我也希望如此。

汤普森：看，这就是我的行李包。

张：我们的车就在外面停车场，我们送您去宾馆。

汤普森：太好了。

Dialogue 3

(At a business meeting)

Chairperson: Okay, I think we should start now. It's ten o'clock.

Voices: Okay/right/yeah.

Chairperson: Well, we're here today to look at some of the reasons for the decline in profits which has affected this subsidiary. You've all seen the agenda. I'd like to ask if anyone has any comments on it before we start?

Voices: No/it's fine/no.

Chairperson: Right, well, can I ask Sam Canning, Chief Sales Executive, to open up with his remarks?

Sam: Thank you, Bernard. Well, I think we have to face up to several realities and what I have to say is in three parts and will talk about twenty minutes.

Chairperson: Er, Sam...We don't have much time—it's really your main points we're most interested in.

Jane: Yes, can I ask one thing, Mr. Chairperson? Isn't this a global problem in our market?

Chairperson: Sorry, Jane, I can't allow us to consider that question yet. We'll look t the global question later. Sam, sorry, please carry on.

Sam: Well, the three points I want to make can be made in three sentences. First, sales are down, but only by 5% more than for the group as a whole. Secondly, our budget for sales has been kept static—it hasn't increased—not even with inflation so we're trying to do better than last year on less money. Thirdly—

Jane: That's not exactly true...

Chairperson: Jane, please. Let Sam finish.

Sam: Thirdly, the products are getting old—we need a new generation.

Chairperson: So let me summarize that. You say sales are down but not by so much, that you've had less money to promote sales and that the products are old? Is that right?

Sam: In a nutshell.

Chairperson: Does anyone have anything to add to that?

Jane: Well, on the question of funding I have to disagree...

主持人：好，我想我们该开始了。现在十点了。

与会者：好的。

主持人：我们今天将要讨论影响我们这个子公司盈利减少的原因。你们都看过会议议程了。在我们开始之前，有人要提出什么意见吗？

与会者：没有。

主持人：好，那么，先有请山姆·坎宁，销售总监，进行开场发言。

山姆：谢谢，伯纳德。我想我们不得不面对某些现状，我想说三方面的问题，大概需要 20 分钟。

主持人：嗯，山姆，我们并没有那么多时间。我们对你想说的要点最感兴趣。

简：对，我能问个问题吗，主持人先生？这不应该是我们市场所面临的总体问题吗？

主持人：对不起，简，我们现在还不能讨论这个问题。之后，我们再来讨论这个总体问题。对不起，山姆，请你继续。

山姆：我想说的三点可以用三句话来概括。首先，销售额的确下降了，但对整体而言只下降了 5 个百分点。其次，我们的预算一直没变，即使在通货膨胀的背景下也没增加。所以我们用的钱比去年少，却要做得更好。最后——

简：并不全是那样……

主持人：简，请让山姆讲完。

山姆：最后，产品正变得陈旧——我们需要开发新一代产品。

主持人：那么让我来总结一下。你说销售额下降但下降得不多，你们在用更少的钱推广产品，产品陈旧了。是这样吗？

山姆：概括得一点不错。

主持人：有人对此有所补充吗？

简：哦，在资金的问题上我不同意……

Supplementary Reading

中国常见商务称谓

Etiquette Guide Helps Make Cubicle Life More Bearable
By David Fusaro

David Vaughan's first day of work at American Airlines in Fort Worth, Texas, was so full of distractions from colleagues in nearby cubicles (小隔间) that he had trouble getting anything done.

"The first day, the first 30 minutes, were crazy with so many interruptions," Vaughan said. "I was like, this can't last too long."

His five years at American, where some 500 workers toil in a 10-acre (英亩) "cube farm," forced him to think hard about the workspace he inhabited. Over drinks one evening, he and a colleague sketched out on a cocktail napkin their idea for a cubicle barrier to restrict unwanted visitors. Vaughan, now 44, and his colleague, Bob Schmidt, eventually left their day jobs with a mission: to change the cube environment. Their first product was Cube Door, which they market online to privacy-starved office workers.

Frustrations like Vaughan's have spawned other innovations and even an etiquette guide intended to make life in a cubicle more palatable (宜人的) and productive. The potential market for products like these is huge: the tens of millions of cube dwellers whose "offices" are separated from their co-workers by 4-foot high fabric-covered walls that create only the impression of privacy.

The cubicle was the brainchild of Bob Probst, a professor at the University of Colorado. Probst was hired by the Herman Miller furniture company in 1964 to research the future of office furniture, according to Joe Schwartz, the company's former marketing head. Probst wanted to create an office space that could be easily modified as companies hired or laid off office workers.

Schwartz said Probst's original plan called for panels connected at 120-degree angles, creating some privacy but also maintaining an open office environment. Schwartz said this set-up was modified over the next several years by interior (室内的) designers and architects, who favored the cube shape to cram as many workers into as small a space as possible.

The end product—a work space both small and public—has tested generations of employees. James Thompson, a former teacher who got his first job in a cubicle when he switched careers three years ago to become a production coordinator at a television network, says he wasn't prepared for office life. He recalls his shock at having to contend with co-workers who treat their cubicles as their own personal space, cutting their nails, passing wind and belching (打嗝).

"It was, in general, a culture shock for me," he said.

That shock prompted Thompson, of Arlington, Va., to write "The Cubicle Survival Guide: Keeping Your Cool in the Least Hospitable Environment on Earth," which was published in March. He has also started a companion blog (thecubiclesurvivalguide.blogspot.com/). The guide offers cube dwellers communal rules, etiquette advice and suggestions for how to deal with violators of the cube compact, said Thompson, 37.

He says he was inspired by a discussion with a co-worker over whether or not it was polite to offer a "bless you" to a colleague who sneezes in the next cubicle. After some discussion, they arrived at the conclusion that a wish of health should be given to anyone in an adjacent cubicle, but a sneeze from two or more cubes away requires no action. They also decided that a guide to cubicle etiquette was necessary.

"The guy next to me said someone really needs to write a code of manners, which many cube communities are sorely lacking," Thompson said.

Some examples of poor etiquette: eating food with a potent (浓烈的) smell, posting inappropriate pictures or post cards and engaging in loud personal phone conversations.

"That's what cell phones are for," Thompson said. "All you have to do is get up and walk away or go outside."

In addition to etiquette rules, the guide offers suggestions for how to fend off co-workers who may be inclined to steal office supplies from cube dwellers who are on vacation or taking a day off. "Office chairs are a really big commodity," Thompson said.

To prevent theft, Thompson suggests cube workers plant a Web cam on the top of their computer. The camera need not be monitored, only left on to present the appearance of a security camera. Or there is what he calls the "Three Mile Island" plan, in which the vacationer leaves crumpled (起皱的) up tissues and a tube of Neosporin (新孢霉素) in a prominent place in his cubicle to make his possessions appear less desirable.

Other stratagems (花招) help the hapless (倒霉的) cube dweller deal with overly nosy (好管闲事的) bosses. Tactics include placing a small mirror on a cubicle wall so that the occupant can see anyone at the entrance of the cube, and installing wireless video baby monitors to keep an eye on foot traffic near the cubicle.

Vaughan and Schmidt have developed their own simple set of privacy devices. As Vaughan looked around his office floor, he noticed co-workers had set up makeshift (临时代用的) barriers with shower curtains and duct tape. He and Schmidt decided there was a need for more aesthetically (美学地) pleasing privacy barriers. So they started CubeSmart, a company that sells simple barriers designed to block the entrance to a cubicle.

The barrier, which costs $35, is essentially a window shade positioned horizontally that can be pulled out across the cube opening when a worker needs privacy. The CubeBanner is a 1/2-foot-tall translucent banner with an American flag logo and a script that reads "I'm busy." The CubeDoor Classic is a polymer (聚合体) mesh (网状物) device with no logo that allows someone approaching the cube to see through it, but increases the illusion of privacy. Finally, they offer the CubeDoor, an opaque (不透明的) barrier that offers the most privacy.

There are some aspects of life in the cube that office workers simply can't avoid, like extremely loud cube neighbors and offensive odors. Although Vaughan says CubeSmart doesn't have any anti-odor devices ready at the moment, they have discussed some possible remedies.

"We've talked about something that maybe looks like a motorcycle helmet (头盔)," Vaughan said, "If you have an all-enclosed stormtrooper (突击队员) type helmet, you could make private phone calls and you wouldn't have to put up with the smells."

Chapter 11
Taboos in Western Culture and Etiquette

禁忌礼仪

在本章中，你将了解到：

- 西方社会的食物禁忌
- 数字禁忌
- 西方人对颜色的禁忌
- 言语禁忌

Intensive Reading

A *taboo* is a strong social ban relating to any area of human activity or social custom that is sacred and forbidden based on moral judgment and sometimes even religious beliefs. The term comes from the Tongan word tabu, meaning set apart or forbidden, and appears in many Polynesian cultures. In those cultures, a *tabu* (or *tapu* or *kapu*) often has specific religious associations. American author Herman Melville, in his first novel *Typee* describes both the origin and use of the word in Polynesian culture. "The word itself (taboo) is used in more than one signification. It is sometimes used by a parent to a child, when in the exercise of parental authority forbids the child to perform a particular action. Anything opposed to the ordinary customs of the islands, although not expressly prohibited is said to be 'taboo.'"

11.1 Taboo Food and Drink

The concept of a food or drink as taboo is almost always formed when an individual does not have exposure to the culture or group of people who consume the food or drink as a regular part of their diet. Taboos are usually formed because cultural beliefs about other aspects of social practice clash with the unfamiliar practices of another culture. Some of the foods considered taboo by one individual may be a regular source of dietary nourishment for other individuals. These preferences may be developed in childhood and followed for the duration of an individual's life.

For some individuals, consuming a certain part of an animal may be considered unacceptable while consuming other parts may be considered acceptable. In other cases, consuming the animal whole is considered not acceptable. These rules are not universal and vary according to social norms, which change over time and place. In some cases, foods considered taboo may be attributed with special meaning. For instance, oysters are considered an aphrodisiac in some areas of the costal United States.

Foods and drinks that are considered taboo among one group of people may be considered a delicacy by another. The development of taboos may have to do with the relative availability of different sources of dietary nourishment. Foods and drinks perceived as taboo by one group of people may come to be viewed this way because of a lack of knowledge of the cultural context in which they are consumed.

11.1.1 Amphibians and Reptiles

Judaism and Islam strictly forbid the consumption of amphibians, such as frogs, and reptiles, such as crocodiles and snakes.

In other cultures, foods such as frog legs are considered as a delicacy, and frogs are raised commercially (in France, Portugal, China, Indonesia, Caribbean and in parts of the USA and India). Rattlesnakes are eaten in certain parts of the Southwestern United States. Crocodile meat is eaten in Australia, Thailand, South Africa, as well as the United States.

11.1.2 Birds

Many cultures have managed to domesticate many species of birds as a food source. However, scavengers such as vultures and crows are avoided as food in many cultures because they are regarded as carriers of disease, unclean, and associated with death.

In North America, while pigeons (as doves) are a hunted game bird, urban pigeons are considered unfit for consumption due to the presumption of uncleanness and the parasites which they may carry.

Swan was at one time a dish reserved for royalty. The English custom of Swan Upping derives from this period. In more modern times, swans have been protected in parts of Europe and America, and eating them is considered unacceptable.

In Western cultures today, most people regard songbirds as backyard wildlife rather than as food. Small songbirds are considered a delicacy in some parts of Europe, as well as in Asia and the Middle East.

11.1.3 Cats and Dogs

Generally in all Western countries eating the meat of any type of animal commonly kept as pets (i.e., dogs and cats) is considered taboo.

According to the ancient Hindu scriptures, dog's meat was regarded as the most unclean (and rather poisonous) food possible. Dog's meat is also regarded as unclean under Jewish and Islamic dietary laws; therefore, both of those religious traditions also discourage its consumption.

11.1.4 Deer

Deer is popular as a dish in Alaska, Norway, Sweden, Finland, Russia, and Canada; but is unusual in the United Kingdom and Ireland. This may relate to the popular culture myth of the reindeer as an assistant to Father Christmas, as opposed to the "cows of the north" vision of the northern countries.

11.1.5 Horse

Horse meat is part of the cuisine of countries as widespread as Japan, France, Germany, and

Kazakhstan; but is a strong taboo in the UK, USA, and other countries with Anglo-Saxon traditions. It is also forbidden by Jewish law, because the horse is not a ruminant, nor does it have cloven hooves.

According to the anthropologist Marvin Harris, some cultures class horse meat as taboo because the horse converts grass into meat less efficiently than ruminants. When the same amount of grass is used for breeding cattle for meat, a cow or a sheep will produce more meat than a horse.

There is also an element of sentimentality, as horses have long enjoyed a close relationship with many humans, on a similar level to household pets. It is notable that, the English language has no widely used term for horse meat, as opposed to four for pig meat (pork, bacon, ham, gammon), three for sheep meat (lamb, hogget and mutton), two for cow meat (beef and veal), and so on. English speaking countries, however, have sometimes marketed horse meat under the euphemism "cheval meat" (cheval being the French for horse).

11.1.6 Insects

Except for certain locusts and related species, insects are not considered Kosher foods which are prepared according to Jewish law. Dietary laws also require that practitioners check food carefully for insects. In Islam, locusts are considered lawful food along with fish that do not require ritual slaughtering.

Western taboos against insects as a food source generally do not apply to honey. Many vegans avoid honey as any other animal product. Some vegans disagree with avoiding honey, on the grounds that nearly all plants are propagated by insects or birds, and the harvesting of them would be similarly exploitative.

11.1.7 Living Animal

Islamic and Judaic law forbids any portion that is cut from a live animal. However, it is considered acceptable to consume live oysters in the Eastern coasts of the United States and in some areas of France. Both Japan and Korea have traditions of consuming live shellfish.

11.1.8 Offal

Steak and Kidney Pie

Offal is the internal organs of butchered animals, and may refer to parts of the carcass such as the head and feet in addition to organ meats such as sweetbreads and kidney. Offal is a traditional part of many European and Asian cuisines, including such dishes as the well-known steak and kidney pie in the UK.

However, in countries such as Australia, Canada, and the United States, many people are disgusted at eating offal. In the US, except for the heart, tongue (beef), liver (chicken, beef, or pork), and intestines used as natural sausage casings, organ meats consumed in the USA tend to be regional or ethnic specialties.

11.1.9 Snails

Land snails have been eaten for thousands of years. They are also seen as a delicacy in China and in several Asian countries along with France, Greece, and other Mediterranean countries.

However, in Britain, Ireland, and the United States, eating land snails is sometimes seen as disgusting. Some English-speaking commentators have used the French word for snails, escargot, as an alternative word for snails, particularly snails for consumption.

Sea snails and even freshwater snails are also eaten in various parts of the world. As they are one species of shellfish, snails are not Kosher food.

11.1.10 Alcohol

Some religions—including Hinduism, Buddhism, Islam, and various branches of Christianity—forbid or discourage the consumption of alcoholic beverages.

Drinking habits are well determined by each culture (as in European and American rules concerning alcoholic beverages) or religious group.

There are also cultural taboos against the consumption of alcohol, reflected for example in the Temperance movement during the 19th and 20th centuries. There is also something of a cultural taboo in several Western countries, including the United States, against the consumption of alcohol by women during pregnancy for health reasons.

11.1.11 Blood

Some religions prohibit drinking blood or eating food made from blood. In Islam, the consumption of blood is prohibited. Halal animals should be properly slaughtered to drain out the blood. Unlike in other traditions, this is not because blood is holy, but simply because blood is considered unclean. In Judaism all mammal and bird meat (not fish) is salted to remove the blood. Since "the life of the animal is in the blood," no person may eat (or drink) the blood.

Drinking blood is a strong taboo in many other countries, and is often vaguely associated with vampirism (the consumption of human blood). According to the *Bible*, blood is only to be used for special or sacred purposes in connection with worship.

However, blood sausage or blood made into cake form, is quite popular in many parts of the world, such as the Philippines, China, Finland, and Britain.

Black Pudding, before cooking

西方社会礼仪与文化

11.2 Taboo Numbers

11.2.1 Thirteen and Friday

In the West, 13 is always regarded as an unlucky number because in the *Bible*, there were 13 diners at the Last Supper before Jesus was betrayed. It is said that if 13 people sit down for dinner together, one will die within the year. The number 13 has been shunned for centuries. Many cities do not have a 13th Street or a 13th Avenue. Many buildings don't have a 13th floor. If you have 13 letters in your name, you will have the devil's luck. Besides, the *Bible* says that Jesus died on a Friday.

Some say Friday's bad reputation goes all the way back to the Garden of Eden. It was on a Friday, supposedly, that Eve tempted Adam with the forbidden fruit. Adam bit and they were both expelled from Paradise. Tradition also holds that the Great Flood began on a Friday; God tongue-tied the builders of the Tower of Babel on a Friday; the Temple of Solomon was destroyed on a Friday; and, of course, Friday was the day of the week on which Christ was crucified. It is therefore a day of penance for Christians.

When the 13th day of a month falls on Friday (Friday the 13th), it will be thought to be a very dangerous day. Some people are so fearful of that day that they avoid their normal routines in doing business, taking flights, or even getting out of bed. It may have been connected to a single catastrophic historical event that happened nearly 700 years ago. The "catastrophe" was the slaughter of the Knights Templar, the legendary order of "warrior monks" formed during the Christian Crusades to combat Islam. Renowned as a fighting force for 200 years, by the 1300s the order had grown so pervasive and powerful it was perceived as a political threat by kings and popes alike and brought down by a church-state conspiracy. Thousands of Knights Templar were arrested and condemned by agents of Philippe IV, King of France, in a "pre-dawn raid" on Friday, October 13th, 1307. In a nutshell, Friday the 13th is a combination of two old superstitions—thirteen is an unlucky number and Friday is an unlucky day.

11.2.2 Six-hundred and Sixty-six

666 is considered to be an evil number in Western culture, especially the Christian world, because the number 666 is named in the *Bible* as the number of the Beast.

> *"Woe to you O earth and sea, for the Devil sends the Beast with wrath, because he knows the time is short. Let him who hath understanding reckon the Number of the Beast, for it is a human number. Its number is six-hundred and sixty-six."*

For centuries, Westerners have been mystified and fascinated by the above passage from the *Book of Revelation*. "The Beast" refers to the Antichrist, who during Earth's last days will unite the world in peace and harmony. However, in order to take part in this prosperity, everyone is required to receive the "Mark of the Beast," presumably the number 666, on their forehead or right hand, in

158 东方剑桥应用英语系列◇◇◇

order to engage in commerce. All of this is actually a plot to convert everyone to the worship of Satan, so that he may triumph over God in the battle between good and evil. To make a long and complicated story short and sweet, Jesus comes down with a horde of angels, a great battle takes place, and God wins the day. Satan and the Beast are cast into the Lake of Fire for eternity, and all their followers are killed.

11.2.3 Odd and Even Numbers

Many Westerners regard even numbers as a symbol of misfortune but odd numbers as a symbol of good luck. According to the doctrine of the Pythagoreans, the unit, or one, was regarded as the father of Numbers, while the duad, or two, was its mother; and thus is explained one source of the general preference for odd numbers. The father was esteemed worthy of greater honor than the mother, and the odd numbers were masculine, while the even numbers were feminine. Moreover, the unit, being the origin of all numbers, represented Divinity, as God was the creator of all things. It was also the symbol of Harmony and Order, whereas the duad signified Confusion and Disorder, and represented the Devil.

Greek historian Plutarch remarks in his *Roman Questions* that the beginning of numbers, or unity, is a divine thing; whereas the first of the even numbers, or Deuce, is directly opposite in character. As for the even number, said this writer, it is defective, imperfect, and indefinite; whereas the uneven or odd number is finite, complete, and absolute.

Therefore, in many areas including Russia, Spain, and Slavic countries, flowers are accepted only in odd numbers at weddings while even numbers are given at funerals.

As for the Westerners, the number seven is considered lucky not only because God used seven days to create the world (to be exact, six, but then one to rest), but also because it is the sum of three and four, which since early Christian times have been believed to be sacred numbers.

11.3 Taboo Colors
11.3.1 Black

Black is a basic taboo color in Western culture, which is often associated with negative connotation.

Black is not a color, strictly speaking. It is the absence of all color. When people speak of opposites, it is usually in terms of black and white. Black, and its opposite white, represent polarities. Black absorbs all aspects of light. While white reveals, black conceals. It has come to mean hidden, fearful or a bad experience. It is linked to the unknown or the unseen. In times of fear and uncertainty, black contains the energy of the threatening unknown. In most Western countries, black is the color of mourning.

11.3.2 Red

Red is a strong color that covers a range of seemingly conflicting emotions from passionate love to violence and warfare. In English culture, red is frequently used as a symbol of guilt, sin, and anger. It is often connected with blood or sex.

Red is the hottest of the warm colors. Studies show that red can have a physical effect on people by increasing the rate of respiration and raising blood pressure. The expression, "seeing red" indicates anger and may stem not only from the stimulus of the color but from the natural flush (redness) of the cheeks, which is a physical reaction to anger, increased blood pressure, or physical exertion.

Red is power, hence the red power tie for business people and the red carpet for celebrities and VIPs (very important person). Flashing red lights denote danger or emergency. Stop signs and stop lights are red to get the drivers' attention and alert them to the dangers of the intersection.

11.3.3 Yellow

Yellow is sunshine. It is a warm color that, like red, has conflicting symbolism. On the one hand it denotes happiness and joy, but on the other hand yellow is the color of cowardice and deceit.

If someone is yellow it means they are a coward, so yellow can have a negative meaning in some cultures.

Because of the high visibility of bright yellow, it is often used for hazard signs and some emergency vehicles. Its use for hazard signs creates an association between yellow and danger, although not quite as dangerous as red.

11.4 Verbal Taboo

Taboo words are in effect banned in polite conversation, in writing, and especially in print. Certain concepts or phrases are taboo on an international level. In general, references to death, bodily effluvia, or sex are considered taboo, as well as blasphemy. Some words are also considered taboo merely because they sound like a taboo word. American linguist J. M. Steadman, Jr. concluded three characteristics of verbal taboo: (1) Coarse, obscene words; (2) words of a sinister or unpleasant suggestion; and (3) innocent words that are or have become contaminated by association with forbidden words.

11.4.1 Taboos on Disease and Death

Due to people's fear of death or disability, words relating to disease and death are normally avoided or treated euphemistically.

For instance, people tend to say "a long disease" instead of "cancer;" or say "pass away," "depart," "be no more," or other expressions instead of "die." Literally hundreds of euphemisms for death may be found. The late Professor Louise Pound collected them in a study of 1936 ranging from the literary to the vulgar. She recorded the legend about the panicked clergyman who said, pointing to the corpse, "This is only the shell, the nut is gone."

However, medical disorders and diseases like cancer, AIDS and suicide aren't as heavily taboo now as in the past.

11.4.2 Sacrilegious Taboos

The Christian culture believes that it is disrespectful for the misuse of God or God's name. References to Hell are also often reproved. Christians are forbidden to "take the lord's name in vain."

Because of a combination of the sense of taboo and the need for expletives, taboo words when used as exclamations have been adapted and softened so as to be less direct, sacrilegious, and offensive. For instance, *God!* becomes *Gosh!*, *Jesus!* is shortened to *Gee!*, *Damn* (*it*)! becomes *Darn* (*it*)!, and *Hell!* becomes *Heck!*.

11.4.3 Abusive Taboos

In most of Europe, Canada, and the United States, charges can be laid for verbal abuse under certain circumstances.

Verbal abuse can occur with or without the use of expletives, including:

(i) Words to make someone feel unimportant;

(ii) saying unkind words about someone's clothes, appearance, race, religion, ethnicity, sexual orientation, and so on;

(iii) and calling someone animal names with abusive meaning, such as bitch, donkey (ass), pig (swine), and cow (an offensive word for women).

11.4.4 Obscene Taboos

Words relating to sex and excrement are also called "four-letter words," such as "fuck" and "piss." The use of *fuck* as an expletive dates only from the early 20th century. *Fuck* itself is first recorded as a verb in 1528 and as a noun in 1663. Both words have German origins and were not taboo words to begin with. What might have happened is that, following the Norman Conquest, French words for bodily parts and functions took the place of the Old English equivalents in respectable contexts, leaving the Old English words to be used in less respectable ones.

Human anatomy has always held an element of taboo for polite society, as Israel historian Norman Rubin describes:

"One of the earliest victims of verbal prudery was the mention of various parts of the body. 'Belly' as early as 1375 was replaced by 'stomach;' and the word 'leg' seems to have engendered more distress than 'belly;' especially in the United States, where even the mention of 'feet' was banned at one time. So 'legs' became 'limb;' 'naked' in the proper English press still remains 'unclothed;' 'bosoms' refer to breast (even breastpin in the USA in 1834 became 'bosom pin'); and at the beginning of the century a 'breast of chicken' was referred to as the 'second wing'..."

With the development of society, we are beginning to observe a progression: Society becomes more tolerant toward a taboo as people continually violate it. None of the above mentioned taboos are taboo to us any longer. The rise of science and rationalism has also reduced the power of many former taboos in modern cultures. For example, today's media serves us an almost limitless supply of things which were formerly taboo—large-scale death, common references to bodily functions, and anatomy. If a taboo is accepted by a culture, then by definition it is no longer a taboo.

◆ Vocabulary ◆

sacred /ˈseikrid/ *a.* worthy of religious veneration 神圣的

Tongan /ˈtɔŋgən/ *a.* of a Polynesian people of Tonga 汤加的

Polynesian /ˌpɔləˈniːʒən/ *a.* of any of the indigenous peoples of Polynesia（包括新西兰、夏威夷、萨摩亚等中太平洋群岛的）波利尼西亚的

aphrodisiac /ˈæfrəuˌdiziæk/ *n.* an aphrodisiac food, drug, potion, or other agent that arouses sexual desire 壮阳剂

perceive /pəˈsiːv/ *v.* to regard as being such 视为，认为

amphibian /æmˈfibiən/ *n.* any cold-blooded vertebrate of the class Amphibia, comprising frogs and toads, newts and salamanders, and caecilians, the larvae being typically aquatic, breathing by gills, and the adults being typically semiterrestrial, breathing by lungs and through the moist, glandular skin 两栖动物

reptile /ˈreptail/ *n.* any of various animals that crawl or creep 爬行动物

Islam /isˈlɑːm/ *n.* the religious faith of Muslims including belief in Allah as the sole deity and in Muhammad as his prophet 伊斯兰教

Caribbean /ˌkæriˈbi(ː)ən/ *a.* of or relating to the Caribs, the eastern and southern West Indies, or the Caribbean Sea 加勒比海的

domesticate /dəˈmestiˌkeit/ *v.* to adapt (an animal or plant) to life in intimate association with and to the advantage of humans 驯化

scavenger /ˈskævəndʒə/ *n.* an organism that typically feeds on carrion 食腐动物

vulture /ˈvʌltʃə/ *n.* any of various large birds that are related to the hawks, eagles, and falcons but have weaker claws and the head usually naked and that subsist chiefly or entirely on carrion 秃鹫

parasite /ˈpærəsait/ *n.* an organism living in, with, or on another organism in 寄生虫

Hindu /ˈhinduː/ *n.* an adherent of Hinduism 信奉印度教的人

ruminant /'ru:minənt/ *n.* a ruminant mammal 反刍动物

cloven hoof /'kləuvən hu:f/ a foot (as of a sheep) divided into two parts at its distal extremity 偶蹄, hoof 的复数形式为 hooves

euphemism /'ju:fə,mizəm/ *n.* the substitution of an agreeable or inoffensive expression for one that may offend or suggest something unpleasant 委婉语

gammon /'gæmən/ *n.* a particular cut of ham and also bacon 腌猪腿

hogget /'hɔgit/ *n.* the meat from a domestic sheep older than a lamb but younger thon one year of age 小羊肉

veal /vi:l/ *n.* the flesh of a young calf 小牛肉

locust /'ləukəst/ *n.* short-horned grasshopper 蝗虫

Kosher /'kəuʃə/ *a.* sanctioned by Jewish law （尤指食物）犹太教所规定允许的

vegan /'vedʒən/ *n.* a strict vegetarian who consumes no animal food or dairy products 严格的素食主义者

propagate /'prɔpəgeit/ *v.* to cause to continue or increase by sexual or asexual reproduction 繁衍

exploitative /iks'plɔitətiv/ *a.* exploiting or tending to exploit 剥削的

offal /'ɔfəl/ *n.* the viscera and trimmings of a butchered animal removed in dressing 内脏

carcass /'kɑ:kəs/ *n.* the dressed body of a meat animal （动物的）尸体

sweetbread /'swi:tbred/ *n.* the thymus or pancreas of a young animal (as a calf) used for food 小牛或小羊的胰脏或胸腺, 杂碎

intestine /in'testin/ *n.* the tubular part of the alimentary canal that extends from the stomach to the anus 肠

escargot /eska:'gəu/ *n.* a snail prepared for use as food 〈法〉食用蜗牛

Buddhism /'budizəm/ *n.* religion of eastern and central Asia growing out of the teaching of Gautama Buddha that suffering is inherent in life and that one can be liberated from it by mental and moral self-purification 佛教

temperance /'tempərəns/ *n.* moderation in or abstinence from the use of alcoholic beverages 戒酒

halal /hə'lɑ:l/ *a.* sanctioned by Islamic law 按伊斯兰教律法合法的

vampirism /'væmpaiərizəm/ *n.* belief in vampires 相信有吸血鬼的迷信

crucify /'kru:sə,fai/ *v.* to put to death by nailing or binding the wrists or hands and feet to a cross 把（某人）钉死在十字架上

penance /'penəns/ *n.* a sacramental rite that is practiced in Roman, Eastern, and some Anglican churches and that consists of private confession, absolution, and a penance directed by the confessor （赎罪的）苦行, 忏悔

shun /ʃʌn/ *v.* to avoid deliberately and especially habitually 避免

catastrophe /kə'tæstrəfi/ *n.* a momentous tragic event ranging from extreme misfortune to utter overthrow or ruin 灾难

Crusade /kru:'seid/ *n.* any of the military expeditions undertaken by Christian powers in the 11st, 12th, and 13th centuries to win the Holy Land from the Muslims 十字军东征

combat /kəmˈbæt/ *v.* to fight with 与……战斗

pervasive /pəˈveisiv/ *a.* existing in or spreading through every part of something 无处不在的

conspiracy /kənˈspirəsi/ *n.* the act of conspiring together 密谋

condemn /kənˈdem/ *v.* to pronounce guilt 宣判(某人)有罪

raid /reid/ *n.* a surprise attack by a small force 突袭

woe /wəu/ *n.* ruinous trouble 灾难, 麻烦

wrath /ræθ/ *n.* strong vengeful anger 盛怒

hath /hæθ/ *v.* archaic present 3rd singular of have 〈废〉have 的第三人称单数现在式

mystify /mistəˌfai/ *v.* to make mysterious or obscure 使困惑

fascinate /ˈfæsineit/ *v.* to transfix and hold spellbound by an irresistible power 慑住……

Revelation /ˌrevəˈleiʃən/ *n.* an apocalyptic writing addressed to early Christians of Asia Minor and included as a book in the *New Testament* 《启示录》(《圣经·新约》的末卷)

prosperity /prɔsˈperiti/ *n.* the condition of being successful or thriving 成功, 昌盛

plot /plɔt/ *n.* secret plan for accomplishing a usually evil or unlawful end 密谋

convert /kənˈvəːt/ *v.* to bring about a religious conversion in 皈依, 改变(信仰)

horde /hɔːd/ *n.* a teeming crowd 一大群

eternity /iˈtəːniti/ *n.* the quality or state of being eternal 永恒

doctrine /ˈdɔktrin/ *n.* a principle or position or the body of principles in a branch of knowledge or system of belief 教义

Pythagorean /paiˌθægəˈriːən/ *n.* any of a group professing to be followers of the Greek philosopher Pythagoras 毕达哥拉斯派

duad /ˈdjuːæd/ *n.* two 成对的东西

masculine /ˈmɑːskjulin/ *a.* having qualities appropriate to or usually associated with a man 男性特有的, 阳性的

feminine /ˈfeminin/ *a.* characteristic of or appropriate or unique to women 女性特有的, 阴性的

deuce /djuːs/ *n.* two points 两点

Slavic /ˈslɑːvik/ *a.* of, relating to, or characteristic of the Slavs or their languages 斯拉夫语的

connotation /ˌkɔnəˈteiʃən/ *n.* the suggesting of a meaning by a word apart from the thing it explicitly names or describes 含义

polarity /pəˈlæriti/ *n.* the particular state either positive or negative with reference to the two poles 对立, 两极化

stimulus /ˈstimjələs/ *n.* something that encourages activity in people or things 刺激物, 兴奋剂

respiration /ˌrespəˈreiʃən/ *n.* a single complete act of breathing 呼吸

exertion /igˈzəːʃən/ *n.* a laborious or perceptible effort 费力

denote /diˈnəut/ *v.* to serve as an arbitrary mark for 象征, 表示

intersection /ˌintəˈsekʃən/ *n.* a place or area where two or more things (as streets) intersect 十字路口

cowardice /ˈkauədis/ *n.* lack of courage or resolution 懦弱

effluvia /iˈfluːvjə/ *n.* an offensive exhalation or smell, plural form for effluvium 臭气

blasphemy /ˈblæsfəmi/ **n.** the act of insulting or showing contempt or lack of reverence for God 亵渎神明(的言行)

coarse /kɔ:s/ **a.** crude or unrefined in taste, manners, or language 粗俗的

obscene /ɔbˈsi:n/ **a.** containing or being language regarded as taboo in polite usage 猥亵的，下流的

sinister /ˈsinistə/ **a.** unfavorable, unlucky 不吉祥的

contaminate /kənˈtæmineit/ **v.** to make unfit for use by the introduction of unwholesome or undesirable elements 玷污

corpse /kɔ:ps/ **n.** dead body especially of a human being （尤指人的）尸体

sacrilegious /ˌsækrəˈlidʒəs/ **a.** of technical and not necessarily intrinsically outrageous violation (as improper reception of a sacrament) of what is sacred because consecrated to God 亵渎神圣的

reprove /riˈpru:v/ **v.** to express disapproval of 谴责

expletive /eksˈpli:tiv/ **n.** an exclamatory word or phrase 感叹词，咒骂语

exclamation /ˌekskləˈmeiʃən/ **n.** vehement expression of protest or complaint 感叹语

abusive /əˈbju:siv/ **a.** using harsh insulting language 辱骂性的

excrement /ˈekskrəmənt/ **n.** waste matter discharged from the body 排泄物

four-letter /ˈfɔ:ˈletə/ **a.** of, relating to, or being four-letter words 庸俗的，下流的

anatomy /əˈnætəmi/ **n.** the human body （人的）身体

prudery /ˈpru:dəri/ **n.** a prudish act or remark 拘谨

◆ Exercises ◆

Ⅰ. Translation

Directions: *In this part there are 10 words or phrases in English. Please translate them into Chinese.*

1. delicacy
2. bacon
3. steak and kidney pie
4. consumption of alcohol
5. blood sausage
6. Last Supper
7. Jesus
8. odd number
9. even number
10. verbal taboo

Ⅱ. Blank filling

Directions: *In this part there is one short passage with several incomplete sentences. Please fill in all the blanks.*

In the West, _____ is always regarded as an unlucky number because in the Bible there were thirteen _____ at the Last Supper before Jesus was betrayed. And the Bible says that Jesus died on a _____. When the thirteenth day of a month falls on Friday, it will be thought to be a very _____ day. It may have been connected to a _____ event that happened nearly 700 years ago. At dawn on Friday, October 13th, 1307, thousands of Knights Templar were arrested by agents of Philippe IV, King of _____, and later to be tortured. In short, Friday the 13th is a combination of two old _____: that thirteen is an unlucky number and that Friday is an _____ day.

III. Essay questions

Directions: *In this part there are two essay questions. Please write the corresponding answer for each question.*

1. Why is horse meat a strong taboo in some cultures?
2. What are the differences and similarities between the Chinese and English concerning the cultural denotation of the color red?

Situational Dialogues

Dialogue 1

(Disagreeing with somebody's classmate)

Li: Hello, Dan.

Dan: Hi, Li.

Li: Do you have a second? I'd like to talk to you about something.

Dan: Sure. What's up?

Li: You probably didn't intend to do this and I'm sure you didn't refer it to me. I heard that you called the Chinese "Chinks." Was that true?

Dan: Oh. I might've done it, but certainly not on purpose.

Li: I knew you wouldn't do that on purpose. You know, as a Chinese American, this kind of thing hurts my feelings.

Dan: I know. And I swear I won't do it again.

Li: Okay. No hard feelings. Friends?

Dan: Sure. Thank you for reminding me.

Li: You're welcome.

李：你好，丹。

丹：你好，李。

李：你有时间吗？我想和你说点儿事。

丹：当然，什么事儿？

李：你可能并不是故意的，我也知道你不是指我，我听说你称呼中国人"中国佬"，是真的吗？

丹：哦，我也有可能说过，但肯定不是故意的。

李：我知道你不是故意的，你知道，作为一个华裔美国人，这种称呼会伤我的感情的。

丹：我知道，我发誓我不会再这样做了。

李：好的，不要有什么隔阂，还是朋友？

丹：当然，谢谢你提醒我。

李：不客气。

Dialogue 2

(Talking about visiting somebody's home)

Jack: Hi, Yang, are you free tomorrow?

Yang: Yeah, what's up?

Jack: Simon's girlfriend called over to see him and Simon wants to have a party in his house.

Yang: Perfect, I know Simon has some great wine.

Jack: Well, I know, it's really mouthwatering. Tomorrow afternoon, 4 o'clock.

Yang: I will be there on time. By the way, shall we take some gifts for them?

Jack: Good idea, but what does she like? She is a girl, you know. I have to rack my brains day and night every January 14th.

Yang: Me too! Can we send her some flowers? Girls always like it.

Jack: Well, I agree with you.

Yang: I'll go to the flower shop opposite our school tomorrow.

Jack: Please remember to buy seven, nine, or eleven bouquets.

Yang: Why? For what?

Jack: Because Simon's sweetheart, Vera Ilynia, is from Russia.

杰克：你好，杨，明天有空吗？

杨：有啊，什么事儿？

杰克：西蒙的女朋友打电话来说要过来看他。西蒙想在家里开个派对。

杨：太好了，我知道西蒙有些好酒。

杰克：我知道，真让人垂涎欲滴。明天下午 4 点。

杨：我会准时到那儿的。顺便问一下，我们要带点礼物去吗？

杰克：好主意。但她喜欢什么呢？她是女孩，你知道，每年 1 月 14 日我都要绞尽脑汁。

杨：我也是！我们送她些花好吗？女孩子总是喜欢花。

杰克：嗯，同意。

杨：那我明天就去学校对面的花店。

杰克：记得要买七朵、九朵或十一朵花啊。

杨：为什么呀？

杰克：因为西蒙的心上人薇拉·伊蕾娜是俄罗斯人。

Supplementary Reading

中国禁忌礼仪

"13" Still Strikes Fear in the Heart
By Anja Tranovich

Jerry Seagel, a realtor (房产经纪人) in Baton Rouge, La., was on the verge of selling an expensive house a few years ago when the young couple threatened to back out of the deal. The street address, they complained, included the number 13.

Seagel went to a local permit office to plead (陈述) his case for an address change. He expected opposition, but the woman behind the counter wasn't surprised. This happens all the time, she said.

As Seagel's experience shows, fear of the number 13, known in medical circles as triskaidekaphobia (黑色星期五恐惧症), can have a real impact on people's lives. Avoidance of the number 13 and the anxiety it produces have measurable economic and even medical consequences.

Developers build around it. Businesses avoid it. Even the US Navy refuses to launch boats on Friday the 13th. But there are some signs that the societal taboo is eroding.

Donald Dossey, a behavioral scientist who wrote a book on the subject, estimates that 8 or 9 million Americans have an acute fear of the number 13. Thirteen percent of Americans said they would be bothered if they were assigned to the 13th floor of a hotel, according to a February Gallup poll. Three-fourths of those said they would ask for another room.

Anxiety around the number appears to be linked to an increase in accidents, according to one study. In 1993, researchers in Britain looked at traffic accidents in West Sussex and found that Friday the 13th was particularly unlucky in one respect: The risk of hospitalization because of a traffic accident increased by as much as 52 percent on that day. The authors' conclusion: "Staying at home is recommended."

Historians say the superstition dates back to the beginning of Christianity. During the Last Supper, "Jesus was betrayed, humiliated and scourged (鞭打) by Judas, the 13th guest, and it was on a Friday, so there's your double whammy (晦气) of aversions ," said Phillips Stevens Jr., a professor of anthropology at the University of Buffalo.

Dossey says the taboo actually predates (早于) Christianity. He cites a story from Norse mythology strikingly similar to the Last Supper: 12 gods in Valhalla, or heaven, sat down to eat when a 13th uninvited guest showed up and killed the God of Kindness by stabbing him with a branch of mistletoe (槲寄生). In the Middle Ages, witches were said to gather in groups of 13; the 13th witch was coven leader and considered demonic (恶魔的).

Any superstition may be reinforced by personal experience, Stevens says. If an action has positive consequences, people try to repeat it; if it has negative results, they try to avoid it. For example, an athlete who has just won a game will probably prepare similarly for the next one. He'll eat the same breakfast, and maybe wear the same socks. Conversely, if a driver gets into an accident, she might forever avoid the street where the accident occurred. This is the basis for the concept of taboo, Stevens says. In the case of the number 13, the personal taboo has become a societal one, further reinforced by popular custom: many buildings don't have a 13th floor, and airports often don't have a 13th gate.

Hollywood movies like "Friday the 13th" perpetuate (固化) the superstition. The movies play on viewers' fears, linking the number to on-screen blood, gore (血污) and the sense of an ever-lurking (始终潜伏着的) threat.

But the superstition may be on the decline. Fewer buildings are skipping the 13th floor. The Hyatt Regency hotel in downtown Tampa, Fla., for example, has a 13th floor and even a 13th room on that floor. David DiSalvo, the hotel's sales manager, says athletes often ask to be moved off the floor, but it isn't an issue for most guests.

Many new hotels in the area also include the 13th floor, he said. Besides, "whether or not you call it a 13th floor," he says, "if a building goes up more than 12 stories, it has a 13th floor."

Other hotel developers, particularly in luck-obsessed Las Vegas, aren't taking any chances.

The Rio All-Suite Hotel and Casino not only skips the 13th floor, it also skips the 4th and 44th, because four is considered an unlucky number in Chinese and in Japanese the number sounds like the word for "death."

Chinese cell phones numbers containing a four are often sold at a far lower price than other numbers, and in Singapore, cars that have a license plate with the number four are hard to resell.

At the Otis Elevator Co., one in six elevators sold lacks the number 13. The company also sells many elevators in Asia without a fourth floor; in Italy, it's the 17th floor that is often missing.

Dossey doesn't think we will shake off these superstitions any time soon. "If builders are moving away from [skipping unlucky numbers] they won't go very fast," Dossey said. "This is ingrained in us. It's almost in our DNA."

Chapter 12
Etiquette of Body Language

体态礼仪

在本章中，你将了解到：
- 手掌在非言语沟通中的影响力
- 对握手的深层分析
- 手臂和腿的姿势在交际中所起的信号作用
- 如何保持眼神交流
- 常见手势语的含义

Intensive Reading

Body language is a form of mental and physical ability of human *non-verbal communication*, which consists of body posture, gestures, facial expressions, and eye movements. Humans send and interpret such signals almost entirely subconsciously, because they are directly linked to their emotional states. In this chapter we will explore four aspects of the etiquette of body language in particular.

12.1 The Power of the Palm

In ancient times, soldiers always used open palms to show that no weapons were being concealed. Today people still hold one or both palms out to the other person, when they want to be open or honest. Like most body language signals, this is a completely unconscious gesture, and it gives you an intuitive feeling that the other person is telling the truth.

What if people are telling a lie? When children are lying or concealing something, they will often hide their palms behind their back. Similarly, a man who wants to conceal his whereabouts might hide his palms in his pockets, or in an arms-crossed position. Although he tries to explain where he was, the hidden palms may give the other person an intuitive feeling that he is not telling the truth. Studies show most people find it difficult to lie with their palms exposed.

One of the least noticed but most powerful body signals is given by the human palm when giving someone directions or commands and in handshaking. According to British interpersonal relationship expert Allan Pease, there are three main palm command gestures, which are the Palm-Up position, the Palm-Down position, and the Palm-Closed-Finger-Pointed position.

The palm facing up is used as a submissive, non–threatening gesture. If you want someone to talk, you can use it as a "handover" gesture to let them know you expect them to talk and you are ready to listen.

When the palm is turned to face downward, you will immediately project authority. The Nazi salute had the palm facing directly down and was the symbol of power and tyranny during World War Ⅱ.

The Palm-Closed-Finger-Pointed is a fist where the appointed finger is used like a symbolic club with which the speaker figuratively beats his listeners into submission. Finger-pointing not only gains the most negative responses from the listeners but makes them hard to recall what the speaker has said. Alternatively, if you squeeze your fingers against your thumb to make an OK type of gesture and talk using this position, you will come across as authoritative, but not aggressive.

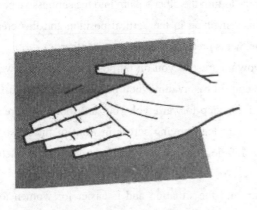

Palm-Up

Hitler's notable Palm-Down gesture

Palm-Closed-Finger-Pointed

Thumb-squeezing

12.2 An Analysis of the Handshake

In Chapter 2 we have talked about the handshake briefly. Now we will make a further analysis. Suppose you have just met someone for the first time and you greet each other with a handshake. Generally you will have one of the three basic attitudes subconsciously.

(i) Submission. "I can dominate this person. He'll do what I want."

(ii) Dominance. "He is trying to dominate me. I'd better be cautious."

(iii) Equality. "I feel comfortable with the person."

In the first case, dominance is transmitted by turning your hand so that your palm faces down in the handshake. Your palm doesn't have to face directly down, but it is the Upper Hand which shows you want to take control of the other person. The opposite of the dominant handshake is to offer your hand with your palm facing upward, symbolically giving the other person the upper hand, which can communicate a submissive attitude. When two dominant people shake hands, a symbolic power struggle takes place as each person attempts to turn the other's palm into the submissive position. The result is a firm handshake with both palms remaining in the vertical position and this creates a feeling of equality and mutual respect because neither is prepared to give in to the other.

If you feel someone is giving a Palm-Down Thrust to you on purpose, here are two ways to disarm them. The first way allows you to take control by invading their personal space but just feels as if you are walking across in front of them. First, step forward with your left foot as you reach to shake hands. Second, step forward with your right leg, moving across in front of the person and into their personal space. Third, bring your left leg across to your right leg to complete the movement, and shake the person's hand.

The other way is a simpler way of dealing with the situation and is easier for women to use. When a power player presents you with a Palm-Down Thrust, respond with your hand in the Palm-Up position, then put your left hand over their right hand to form a Double-Hander, and straighten the handshake.

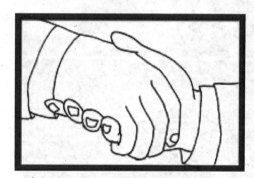

The Dominant Handshake   The Double-Hander

12.3 Arm and Leg Signals

12.3.1 Arm Signals

Hiding behind a barrier is a normal response we learn at an early age to protect ourselves. As children, we hid behind tables, chairs, furniture, our mother's skirt, etc., whenever we found ourselves in a threatening situation. As we grew older, this hiding behavior became more complicated. When it was unacceptable to hide behind solid objects, we learned to fold our arms. By folding one or both arms across the chest, a barrier is formed that is an unconscious attempt to block out what we regard as a threat or undesirable circumstances. Gestures show the corresponding attitudes. Folded arms will make you feel comfortable if you have a negative, defensive, or nervous attitude. However, if you have fun with your friends, folded arms will feel odd.

There are many arm-folding positions. Crossed-Arms-on-Chest is universal and contains the same negative or defensive meaning almost everywhere. When you see someone take the arms-crossed position, it is reasonable to assume that you may have said something with which

Crossed-Arms-on-Chest

they disagree. It may be meaningless to continue your argument even though the person could be verbally agreeing with you. The fact is that body language is more honest than words.

A simple but effective way of breaking the arms-folded position is to give the listener something to hold or give them something to do. For instance, giving them a pen, book, sample, or written material forces them to unfold their arms and lean forward. This turns them into a more open position and therefore a more open attitude. In dealing with the situation, you could ask the listener to lean forward to look at a visual presentation, or you could lean forward yourself with your palms up and say, "What's your opinion?" or something like that. Then you lean back to indicate it is their turn to speak. By using your palms, you nonverbally tell them that you would like them to be open and honest just as what you are being.

12.3.2 Leg Signals

The farther away from the brain a body part is positioned, the less awareness we have of what it is doing. This means after our face, we are less aware of our arms and hands, then our chest and stomach, and we are the least aware of our legs and feet. Legs and feet are an important source of information about someone's attitude because most people are unaware of what they are doing with them.

The legs of ancient people mainly served two purposes: To move forward to get food and to run away from danger. We can judge a person's commitment to leaving or staying in a conversation from their legs. Open or uncrossed leg positions show an open or dominant attitude while crossed positions reveal closed attitudes or uncertainty.

According to Allan Pease, there are four main standing positions:

(i) The Attention Stance

This is a formal position that shows a neutral attitude with no commitment to stay or go. Keep the legs together like a "No Comment" signal.

(ii) The Crotch Displayer

This is a predominantly male gesture and is like a standing Crotch Display. The Crotch Displayer plants both feet firmly on the ground, making a clear statement that he has no intention of leaving.

(iii) The Foot-Forward Position

The body weight is shifted to one hip, which leaves the front foot pointing forward. This is a valuable clue to a person's immediate intentions, because we point our lead foot in the direction our mind would like to go, and this stance looks as if the person is beginning to walk. In a group discussion, we point our lead foot at the most interesting or attractive person. When we want to leave, we point our feet at the nearest exit.

(iv) The Leg-Cross Position

While open legs can show openness or dominance, crossed legs show a closed, submissive, or defensive attitude. Crossing the legs not only reveals negative or defensive emotions, it makes a person appear insecure and causes others to react accordingly.

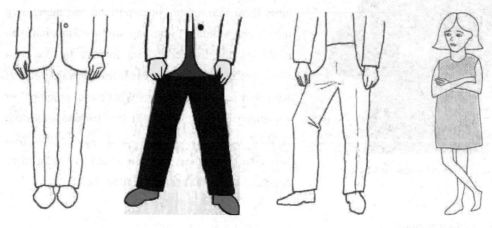

The Attention Stance   The Crotch Displayer   The Foot-Forward Position   The Leg-Cross Position

12.4 Eye Contact

We have been preoccupied with the eyes and their effect in human behavior throughout history. In daily life we spend much of our face-to-face time looking at the other person's face, so eye signals are a vital part of being able to read a person's attitude and thoughts.

Making eye contact is a real basis for establishing communication. While some people can make us feel comfortable when they talk with us, others make us feel ill at ease and some seem untrustworthy. In fact, this has to do with the length of time they look at us or with how long they hold our gaze as they speak.

Michael Argyle, British pioneer of social psychology and nonverbal communication skills, found that when Westerners talk, their average gaze time is 61 percent. 41 percent of gaze time occurs when talking, 75 percent occurs when listening, and 31 percent is mutual gazing. He also recorded the average gaze length to be 2.95 seconds, and the length of a mutual gaze was 1.18 seconds.

When two people meet and make eye contact for the first time, it's usually the person with lower status who looks away first. This means that not looking away becomes a subtle way to deliver a challenge or show disagreement when someone gives their opinion.

In terms of gazing area on one's face, Allan Pease summarizes three basic types of gazing which can dramatically affect the outcome of a face-to-face communication. The first is Social Gazing, which is the area of the face we look at in a nonthreatening environment. The second is Intimate Gazing. When people approach each other from a distance, they look quickly between the other person's face and lower body to first establish what the sex of the person is and then a second time to determine a level of interest in them. In close encounters, it is the triangular area between the eyes and the chest, and for distant gazing, it is from the eyes to the groin or below. The last is called Power Gazing. Imagine the person has a third eye in the center of their forehead and look in a triangular area between a person's "three" eyes. This gaze can change the atmosphere to be very serious. Never use it in friendly or romantic encounters. It works as a threat on the person whom you want to intimidate or on the person who simply won't shut up.

It is not difficult to maintain eye contact with one or two persons, but how to hold eye contact with a large audience? In groups of up to 50 people, it is impossible to meet the gaze of everyone. In larger groups, when you stand at a distance of 30 feet from the front row, peg a real or imaginary point or person at each corner of the group and one in center. In doing so, about 20 people in a group of up to 50 will feel you are looking at them individually as you speak, and you can create an intimate bond with most of your audience.

To keep control of where a person in the audience is looking when you make a presentation, you can use a pen to point to the presentation, and at the same time, verbalize what they see. Next, lift the pen from the presentation and hold it between their eyes and your eyes. This has the magnetic effect of lifting the audience's head so that now they are looking at you and they see and hear what you are saying. This achieves the maximum absorption of your message. Keep the palm of your other hand open when you are speaking.

The Social Gaze Zone

The Intimate Gaze Zone

The Power Gaze Zone

12.5 Single Hand Gestures

Gestures play a major role in many aspects of human life. No society is reported without gestures. Gestures are culture-specific and can convey very different meanings in different social or cultural settings. As we have mentioned some gestures in the above sections, here we will discuss other single hand gestures which are commonly seen in the West.

(i) Beckoning Gesture

The Beckoning Gesture in North America is only used for dogs in the Philippines.

In North America or Northern Europe, a beckoning gesture is made with the index finger sticking out of the clenched fist, palm facing the gesturer. The finger moves repeatedly towards the gesturer as to draw something nearer. It has the general meaning of "come here." However, in several European countries, a beckoning gesture is made with a scratching motion with all four fingers and with the palm down.

(ii) Crossed Fingers

Crossed fingers are used to superstitiously wish for good luck or to nullify a promise.

(iii) High Fives

The high five is a celebratory hand gesture that occurs when two people simultaneously raise one hand about head high, and they push, slide, or slap the flat of their palm and flat hand against the palm and flat hand of their partner. The gesture is often preceded verbally by the phrase "Give me five" or "High five."

(iv) Horns Gesture

This is a hand gesture with a variety of meanings and uses in various cultures. It is formed by extending the index and little fingers while holding the middle and ring fingers down with the thumb. When confronted with unfortunate events, or simply when these are mentioned, the sign of the horns may be given to ward off bad luck. However, in some Mediterranean countries such as Portugal, Spain, and Italy, the sign of horns has a vulgar meaning which is used to indicate a man's wife is unfaithful. It is also used in rock and roll, especially in heavy metal music. While in the USA, this gesture is the logo for the Texas University, which represents the Texas Longhorn mascot.

Crossed Fingers

High Fives

Horns Gesture

(v) ILY Gesture

The ILY gesture combines the letters "I," "L," and "Y," from American Sign Language by extending the thumb, index finger, and pinky finger while the middle and ring finger touch the palm. It is an informal expression of love.

(vi) OK Gesture

The OK gesture is made by connecting the thumb and forefinger in a circle and holding the other fingers straight. It is a signal of the word "okay."

(vii) Phone Gesture

The phone gesture is made by outstretching the thumb and pinky finger with the other fingers tight against the palm. The thumb goes to the ear and pinky finger to the mouth as though they were a telephone receiver. It is used to say, "I'll call you," to request a future telephone conversation, or to tell someone of a call.

(viii) The Finger

This is an obscene hand gesture often meaning the phrases: "Up yours," "fuck off," or "screw you." It is performed by showing the back of a closed fist that has only the middle finger extended upwards.

 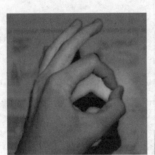  

ILY Gesture   OK Gesture   Phone Gesture   The Finger

(ix) The Thumbs-Up

In places that have strong British influence, such as Australia, the USA, Singapore, and New Zealand, the Thumbs-Up gesture has three meanings: It is commonly used by hitchhikers who are requesting a ride in an automobile; it is an OK signal; and when the hand and thumb are jerked sharply upward it becomes an insult, meaning "up yours." In some countries such as Greece, the thumb is thrust forward and its main meaning is "get stuffed."

(x) V Gesture

The V gesture is a hand gesture in which the index and middle fingers are raised and parted, while the other fingers are clenched. It has various meanings, depending on the cultural context and how it is presented. It is most commonly used to represent the letter V as in "victory," as a symbol of peace (usually with palm outward), as an offensive gesture (palm inward), and to represent the number two. In the United Kingdom, Australia, New Zealand, and Ireland, you should avoid making this gesture with the back of your hand facing the observer.

The Thumb-Up

V Gesture (Palm outward)

◆ Vocabulary ◆

subconsciously /ˌsʌbˈkɒnʃəsli/ *ad.* from the subconscious mind 潜意识地

conceal /kənˈsiːl/ *v.* prevent from being seen or discovered 掩饰, 隐藏

intuitive /inˈtuːitiv/ *a.* spontaneously derived from or prompted by a natural tendency 直觉的

submissive /səbˈmisiv/ *a.* inclined or willing to submit to orders or wishes of others or showing such inclination 顺从的

thrust /θrʌst/ *n.* a sharp hand gesture (resembling a blow) 推力 *v.* push forcefully 猛推

project /prəˈdʒekt/ *v.* communicate vividly (使)展现

authority /ɔːˈθɔriti/ *n.* freedom from doubt; belief in yourself and your abilities 权威, 威信

salute /səˈluːt/ *n.* formal military gesture of respect 敬礼

tyranny /ˈtirəni/ *n.* dominance through threat of punishment and violence 专横, 暴行

club /klʌb/ *n.* stout stick that is larger at one end 棍棒

figuratively /ˈfigjərətivli/ *ad.* in a figurative sense 形象地, 比喻地

aggressive /əˈgresiv/ *a.* having or showing a quality of anger and determination that makes them ready to attack other people 好斗的, 挑衅的

dominate /ˈdɔmineit/ *v.* be in control 控制, 支配

transmit /trænzˈmit/ *v.* send from one person or place to another 传递, 传达

crotch /krɔtʃ/ *n.* the angle formed by the inner sides of the legs where they join the human trunk 胯部

predominantly /priˈdɔminəntli/ *ad.* much greater in number or influence 占主导地位地

preoccupied /priːˈɔkjəˌpaid/ *a.* having or showing excessive or compulsive concern with something 全神贯注的

groin /grɔin/ *n.* the crease at the junction of the inner part of the thigh with the trunk together with the adjacent region and often including the external genitals 腹股沟

intimidate /in'timideit/ *v.* make timid or fearful 恐吓，威胁

peg /peg/ *v.* fasten or secure with a wooden pin 用钉子固定

verbalize /'və:bəlaiz/ *v.* express in speech 用言语描述

magnetic /mæg'netik/ *a.* possessing an extraordinary ability to attract 有吸引力的

clench /klentʃ/ *v.* squeeze together tightly 握紧

scratch /skrætʃ/ *v.* scrape or rub as if to relieve itching 搔痒

superstitiously /ˌsju:pə'stiʃəsli/ *ad.* in a superstitious manner 迷信地

nullify /'nʌləˌfai/ *v.* show to be invalid 使抵消，使无效

simultaneously /saiməl'teiniəsli/ *ad.* at the same instant 同时地

vulgar /'vʌlgə/ *a.* conspicuously and tastelessly indecent 粗俗的

mascot /'mæsˌkɔt/ *n.* a person or animal that is adopted by a team or other group as a symbolic figure 吉祥物

pinky /'piŋki/ *n.* the finger farthest from the thumb 小指

hitchhiker /'hitʃˌhaikə/ *n.* a person who travels by getting free rides from passing vehicles 搭便车的旅行者

jerk /dʒə:k/ *v.* pull, or move with a sudden movement 猛拉

◆ **Exercises** ◆

Ⅰ. **Translation**

Directions: *In this part there are 10 words or phrases in English. Please translate them into Chinese.*

1. Palm-Up
2. Palm-Down
3. Double-Hander
4. Crossed-Arms-on-Chest
5. Attention Stance
6. Crotch Displayer
7. gaze zone
8. beckoning gesture
9. index finger
10. ring finger

Ⅱ. **Blank filling**

Directions: *In this part there is one short passage with several incomplete sentences. Please fill in all the blanks.*

In terms of gazing area on one's face, British interpersonal relationship expert, Allan Pease, summarizes three basic types of gazing which can dramatically affect the outcome of a face-to-face communication. The first is _____, which is the area of the face we look at in a non–threatening environment. The second is _____. When people approach each other from a distance, they look quickly between the other person's face and lower body to first establish what the _____ of the person is and then a second time to determine a level of interest in them. In close encounters, it is the triangular area between the eyes and the _____, and for distant gazing, it is from the _____ to the groin or below. The last is called _____. Imagine the person has a third eye in the center of their forehead and look in a _____ area between a person's "three" eyes. This gaze can change the atmosphere to be very _____.

III. Essay questions

Directions: *In this part there are two essay questions. Please write the corresponding answer for each question.*

1. How would you transmit the feeling of equality and friendliness through a handshake, arm and leg signals, as well as eye contact? Illustrate them respectively.

2. Can you list and explain some single hand gestures which are commonly seen in the West?

Situational Dialogues

Dialogue 1

(Talking about gesture at a restaurant)

Liu: Mr. Kasper, do you like Chinese tea?

Kasper: Yeah, of course, I like it very much. I even often have it after dinner.

Liu: Do you? We Chinese have very complicated tea drinking gestures.

Kasper: I heard some of them. I am very impressed.

Liu: Could you please tell me the gestures in business in Western countries?

Kasper: You know I am not very professional, but I can tell you some in the US.

Liu: That's good.

Kasper: In our culture, Americans are "not touch" oriented. In normal social situations, Americans generally stand about 30 inches apart from one another, which is also considered their personal "comfort zone." Gestures are quite simple. When greeting one another, Americans shake hands. From an early age they are taught to do so with a firm and solid grip.

Liu: We do the same in China, but not firmly especially when shaking hands with ladies and the elderly. Besides, a nod of the head or slight bow is also applied. Hugging and kissing when greeting are uncommon.

Kasper: Yeah. I know that. I also noticed that public displays of affection are very rare in China. You may also note people of the same sex walking hand-in-hand, which is simply a gesture of friendship. But in our culture, it is quite rare; in many cases, it signals homosexuality.

Liu: I do not know much about gestures in your country. I remembered in your movies, people extend the forefinger and make a circular motion near the temple or ear. What does this gesture mean?

Kasper: It means something or someone is "crazy." In Argentina, it means "you have telephone call."

Liu: Oh, I thought it meant "thinking" or "using your mind."

Kasper: Aha, no, no, no. That's cultural misunderstanding. There are some gestures with different meanings. For instance, a palm facing out with the index and middle fingers displayed in the shape of a "V": This gesture means VICTORY in our culture, but in England, a palm facing inward toward the face is an obscene gesture.

Liu: I thought you had very similar culture, but you are so different concerning this gesture.

Kasper: You got it. We often use the OK gesture to mean "fine" or "yes," but in France, it means zero. In Japan, it means money or coins. In Brazil, Germany, and the former USSR, it is an obscene gesture.

Liu: Very interesting. People in the world are so different!

刘：卡斯朋先生，你喜欢中国的茶吗？

卡：是的，当然，我非常喜欢。我经常用餐之后会喝一杯。

刘：是吗？我们中国人的喝茶手势非常复杂呢。

卡：我听说过一些，印象很深刻。

刘：你可以告诉我西方国家商务场合中的一些手势语吗？

卡：你知道我不是专家，但我可以告诉你美国的情况。

刘：好的。

卡：在我们的文化中，美国不是"接触"型文化。在平常的社交场合中，美国人通常站在距离别人30英寸之外的地方，他们称之为个人的"适宜范围"。手势也很简单。当和别人打招呼时，美国人会握手，在他们年幼时就被教导握手要有力、结实。

刘：在中国也是一样，不过在和女士和老人握手时不可以太用力。此外，我们也常用点头示意，或者轻轻地鞠躬来打招呼。见面时拥抱、接吻不常见。

卡：对，这个我知道。我也注意到在中国，人们很少在公共场合示爱。你可能也发现了有些同性的人牵着手同行，那显示了他们的友情。但是在我们的文化中，这样的做法比较少见。在很多情况下，手牵手同行表示两人是同性恋关系。

刘：我对你们国家的手势语不太了解。我记得在你们的电影中，人们会伸出食指在太阳穴或耳朵那里绕一圈，那是什么意思？

卡：意思是某件事或某个人很"疯狂"。在阿根廷，这个手势的意思是"你有来电"。

刘：噢，我还以为那表示"思考"或"用用你的大脑"呢！

卡：哈哈，不是的，不是的。那是对文化的误读。有些手势具有不同的意思。比如，手掌朝外无名指和中指摆出"V"字形，在我们的文化中是"胜利"的意思。但在英格兰，如果手掌朝内对着脸部，则是一个下流的姿势。

刘：我还以为你们的文化很相似呢，可是你们在对这个姿势的解读上是如此不同。

卡：是啊！往往"OK"这个手势表示"好"或者"是的"。但在法国，它却是零的意思。在日本，它代表钱或者硬币。在巴西，德国和前苏联，它又是一个很下流的手势。

刘：真有趣！世界上的人真是迥异！

Dialogue 2

(Talking about eye contact in business communication)

White: Hi, Mr. Jin, could you come to my office for a while?

Jin: Sure.

(Jin gets into Mr. White's office.)

White: Take a seat.

Jin: Thank you very much.

White: Yeah, you did a great job yesterday. Our client Mr. Johnson praised you a lot for your quick reaction and excellent interpretation.

Jin: Oh, did he? I'm so honored.

White: Yeah, you deserve it and I absolutely agree with him. However, there is one thing he felt a bit uneasy about in the negotiation.

Jin: Oh, really? I hope it is not very serious.

White: Well, one's feeling is very important. I am saying this because I think you have great potential in the business if you improve yourself further in your communication skills.

Jin: Thank you very much. Then, would you please tell me what the matter is?

White: Ah, Mr. Johnson said you did not have good eye contact in the meeting, and he could not understand you at times.

Jin: Really? I'm so sorry about that. To be honest, I did not learn much about eye contact and I even did not even realize that it would influence the communication.

White: Yeah, that's the problem of face-to-face communication. You know, the eyes are said to be the window to the soul—and they can reveal the deeper meaning behind the spoken word.

Jin: Yes, I heard of it.

White: But the amount of proper eye contact varies greatly from culture to culture. You know, the eyes always send proper messages to the people you communicate with.

Jin: Really? Interesting. I'd like to know about it some more.

White: For example, Americans take direct eye contact as a sign of honesty and sincerity. It shows interest and attentiveness, while a lack of eye contact is taken as a sign of untruthfulness.

Jin: Then what about Asian people?

White: From my observation, just like your behavior yesterday, I think you have less eye contact when you communicate. This often happens in the meetings with the Japanese. I think that is the problem for Mr. Johnson.

Jin: I see, you mean you want me to have more eye contact with other people in the future.

White: That's right.

Jin: I will.

White: Remember, don't stare or gaze at others, otherwise, they will think you are demonstrating your aggressiveness.

Jin: I know.

White: Great!

怀特先生：你好，金先生，你能来一下我的办公室吗？

金：当然。

(金来到怀特先生的办公室。)

怀：请坐。

金：非常感谢。

怀：你昨天表现得很好。我们的客户约翰逊先生对你的快速反应和出色的翻译大加赞赏。

金：哦，真的吗？我感到很荣幸。

怀：是啊，你值得他的夸奖，我完全赞同他。但是，在谈判过程中有件事让他感觉有点不安。

金：这样啊？我希望问题不是很严重。

怀：呃，一个人的感觉很重要。我这么说是因为我觉得如果你进一步提高沟通技巧的话，你在商务领域会有很大的潜力。

金：非常感谢。那么你能告诉我问题出在哪里吗？

怀：呃，约翰逊先生说在开会过程中你的眼神沟通不是很好，他有时不太了解你。

金：是吗？我很抱歉。说实话，我对眼神沟通不是很了解，我甚至没有意识到它会影响到双方的交流。

怀：是啊，这就是面对面沟通的一个问题。你知道，眼睛被认为是心灵的窗户——眼睛能够揭示语言背后更深层的含义。

金：是的，我听说过这种说法。

怀：但是眼神沟通的频率随着文化的不同而有很大的差异。你知道，眼神沟通总会向沟通的对方传递适当的信息。

金：真的吗？有意思，我倒想了解了解。

怀：比如说，美国人认为直接的眼神交流是诚实和直率的象征，这种眼神表明感兴趣和关注。而缺少眼神沟通、躲闪的眼神则被认为是不诚实的信号。

金：那么，亚洲人的情况怎么样？

怀：就我的观察来看，就像你昨天的表现一样，我认为你和与会者的眼神交流较少，这种情况在和日本人开会时也会发生。我想这就给约翰逊先生造成困扰了。

金：我知道了。你的意思是让我以后多跟其他的与会者有更多的眼神沟通。

怀：没错。

金：以后我会的。

怀：记住，别凝视或盯着别人看，要不然别人会认为你在挑衅呢。

金：我知道了。

怀：太好了！

Supplementary Reading

中国体态礼仪

What Doctors Are Telling Us Even When They're Not Talking
By Pauline W., Chen M. D.

I recently read through a study published in *The Journal of General Internal Medicine* on the different ways that African-American and white doctors communicate nonverbally with older patients, and I was reminded of a former colleague, a specialist in brain tumors (肿瘤) who stood out from the rest of us young doctors for two reasons.

First, though a relative newcomer to the hospital, he had diagnostic skills equal to those of physicians many years his senior. Second, and not unusual for over a decade ago, he was one of the few African-American physicians there.

One day I asked him to see one of my patients who had recently been given a cancer diagnosis. The patient, who was older and white, was sitting upright in his bed, surrounded by his wife and children, when we entered the room. But by the time we left, the patient, along with his relatives, was doing exactly what I was—leaning over and politely straining (竭力听或看) to hear what my colleague was saying.

This brilliant doctor's soft baritone (男中音) voice was rendered even less comprehensible because he tilted his head down and spoke not toward us but at the door. Every so often he looked up and shared a radiant (喜悦的), even reassuring smile. But then he would look down again, shift his weight and continue speaking too softly to be intelligible.

What puzzled me was that I didn't normally think of this colleague as being that self-effacing (谦卑的). But when I described his visit a couple of days later to another colleague, a mutual friend, she immediately recounted a similar episode. "It's weird, isn't it?" she said. "He's the smartest doctor in the hospital, but when he starts talking to some patients, it's like he's trying to disappear."

For nearly two decades, teaching good communication skills has been mandatory (强制的) for medical schools because of research showing that good patient-doctor communication can lead to improved patient satisfaction and better health care outcomes. To this end, medical educators have developed a host of communication courses and workshops that combine lectures, self-assessments, video recordings and "standardized patients," or actors in the role of patients.

More recently, many schools have broadened their courses to include "cultural competency," or the ability to communicate with those from different racial, ethnic and social backgrounds. Studies have shown that while a patient's race and ethnicity can be linked to sharply different treatment courses and quality, better communication between doctors and patients of different backgrounds can reduce the disparities (悬殊).

Despite these tremendous (巨大的) efforts, there is one area of communication to which few schools have devoted significant time or resources: body language and facial expressions.

Now a small but growing body of research is revealing that the nonverbal component of the patient-doctor interaction—the subtle gestures, body positions, eye contact, touch and expressions that pass between individuals—is as critical a part of communication as verbal expressions. And nonverbal cues may, in fact, be more reflective of the biases (偏见) faced by doctors and patients.

In this recent study, for example, a group of medical sociologists analyzed the interactions between 30 primary care doctors and more than 200 patients over age 65 and found that white physicians tended to treat older patients similarly, regardless of race. Black physicians, on the other hand, often gave white patients contradictory (矛盾的) signals, mixing positive nonverbal behaviors, like prolonged (长时间的) smiling or eye contact, with negative ones, like creating physical barriers by crossing the arms or legs.

The finding was reminiscent (使人想起相似的人或物的) of earlier studies on interactions between female doctors and male patients, in which the doctors tended to give the patients conflicting nonverbal cues, combining, for example, smiles with a negative or anxious tone of voice. These mixed signals, said Irena Stepanikova, the lead author of the recent study and an assistant professor of sociology at the University of South Carolina in Columbia, are a result of dealing with "a status in our society that is devalued (贬低)." Rather than being expressed explicitly (清楚地), biases regarding race and gender tend to be expressed "in behaviors not consciously controlled," she said.

The researchers also found that despite the contradictory cues, the black doctors were generally more skillful in using positive nonverbal behaviors than their white colleagues. They were, for example, better able to use prolonged eye contact, more open body positions, facial expressions and even light touch to encourage patients and convey respect, understanding, availability (有效性) and attention. "Patients feel vulnerable (感情脆弱的) and search for nonverbal cues," Dr. Stepanikova noted. "If the doctor nods when the patient is talking but keeps looking at the chart, the patient will wonder if the doctor is really taking her seriously."

Dr. Stepanikova and her colleagues believe that greater emphasis on nonverbal communication can help medical educators address some of the social biases that affect patient care. But they acknowledge that the process will be challenging. Research in this area is still relatively sparse (稀少的), and few medical educators are well versed (精通) in this topic. Moreover, even experts like Dr. Stepanikova, who needed to devote several hours to analyzing just portions of a single patient-doctor visit, are unsure of how researchers and educators can measure the nuances (细微差别) and complexities of nonverbal communication accurately, consistently and efficiently.

"We all want to be as egalitarian (平等主义的) as possible," Dr. Stepanikova said. "But what is difficult is knowing what and when to change, because so much of nonverbal communication happens outside of our conscious awareness."

Keys to Exercises

Chapter 1

I. Translation

1. 波斯湾战争   2. 文化逻辑   3. 行为模式   4. 亚里士多德逻辑学
5. 三段论   6. 思维模式   7. 同一性/身份   8. 神学教育
9. 礼仪   10. 社会交往

II. Blank filling

behavior, cultural traditions, subculture, cultural universals, shared

Chapter 2

I. Translation

1. 称谓语   2. 泛称   3. 亲属称谓   4. 拟亲属称谓
5. 头衔   6. 当面交流   7. 姓   8. 眼神接触
9. 握手   10. 吻面礼

II. Blank filling

pronoun, noun, kinship terms, Mr./Mrs./Miss/Ms., titles

Chapter 3

I. Translation

1. 女士优先   2. 提供服务   3. 谢绝邀请   4. 预约
5. 感谢信   6. 乔迁聚会   7. 分机号码   8. 留言
9. 别挂机   10. 帮忙

II. Blank filling

Please, Thank you, Sorry, Excuse me, please, thank you, Sorry, Excuse me, sorry, burping, sneezing, Excuse me

Chapter 4

I. Translation

1. 敬请回复。　　　2. 若因故缺席，敬请告知。　　　3. 宴会请柬
4. 答复卡　　　5. 邮政编码　　　6. 签名档　　　7. 回函地址
8. 主题栏　　　9. 密件抄送栏　　　10. 传真封页

II. Blank filling

outer, full name, inner, and guest, bride, reception card, card, deadline

Chapter 5

I. Translation

1. 个人空间　　　2. 靠右行　　　3. 短信　　　4. 搬运工
5. 侍者　　　6. 引座员　　　7. 谢幕　　　8. 起立鼓掌
9. 公共交通　　　10. 靠窗的座位

II. Blank filling

Passage 1: intimate, social, personal space, keep to the right, apologize, Excuse me, queuing

Passage 2: restaurants, fifteen to twenty, bill, one to two, luggage, two, two

Chapter 6

I. Translation

1. 开胃菜　　　2. 主菜　　　3. 公匙　　　4. 抹黄油的小刀
5. 叉尖　　　6. 餐巾　　　7. 甜点　　　8. 自助餐
9. 主宾　　　10. 各自付账

II. Blank filling

Passage 1: outside, farthest, right, dinner knife, plate, top

Passage 2: cupped, palm, bowl, stem, red, cool

Chapter 7

I. Translation

1. 白领结　　　2. 黑领结　　　3. 晨礼服　　　4. 商务套装
5. 燕尾晚礼服　6. 无尾晚礼服　7. 大晚礼裙　　8. 小晚礼裙
9. 女式衬衫　　10. 连裤袜

II. Blank filling

semi-formal, white tie, black tie, morning dress, stroller

Chapter 8

I. Translation

1. 新娘送礼会　2. 主伴郎　　3. 未婚主伴娘　4. 结婚典礼
5. 婚宴　　　　6. 主婚人　　7. 男傧相　　　8. 女傧相
9. 持戒指的男孩　10. 女花童

II. Blank filling

fifteen, mobile phone, procession, bride, officiant, groomsmen, mothers, front

Chapter 9

I. Translation

1. 吊丧　　　　2. 殡仪馆　　3. 抬棺人　　　4. 棺材
5. 悼词　　　　6. 逝者　　　7. 追悼仪式　　8. 入葬仪式
9. 献花　　　　10. 吊唁卡

II. Blank filling

visitation, funeral home, sympathy, deceased, coffin, prayer, full

Chapter 10

I. Translation

1. 国庆日   2. 准时   3. 名片   4. 客户
5. 闲聊   6. 企业标识   7. 主席   8. 设定议程
9. 招聘人员   10. 求职

II. Blank filling

head, power seat, key customer, right, left, across, rectangular

Chapter 11

I. Translation

1. 佳肴   2. 熏肉   3. 牛肉腰子馅饼   4. 酒消费
5. 血肠   6. 最后的晚餐   7. 耶稣   8. 奇数
9. 偶数   10. 言语禁忌

II. Blank filling

thirteen, diners, Friday, dangerous, historical, France, superstition, unlucky

Chapter 12

I. Translation

1. 掌心向上   2. 掌心向下   3. 双手相握   4. 双臂交叉抱胸
5. 立正站姿   6. 显胯站姿   7. 注视区域   8. 召唤手势
9. 食指   10. 无名指

II. Blank filling

Social Gazing, Intimate Gazing, sex, chest, eyes, Power Gazing, triangular, serious

Bibliography

[1] Alan Flusser. *Dressing the Man: Mastering the Art of Permanent Fashion*[M]. New York: Harper Collins，2002.

[2] Allan & Babara Pease. *The Definitive Book of Body Language*[M]. New York: Bantam Books，2006.

[3] Arthur Inch, Arlene Hirst. *Dinner Is Served*[M]. London: Running Press Book Publishers，2003.

[4] Cele C. Otnes, Elizabeth H. Pleck. *Cinderella Dreams: The Allure of the Lavish Wedding*[M]. California: University of California Press，2003.

[5] Conrad Phillip Kottak. *Anthropology: The Exploration of Human Diversity*[M]. Michigan: McGraw Hill Higher Education，2006.

[6] Edward T. Hall. *The Hidden Dimension*[M]. New York: Anchor Books，1990.

[7] Erving Goffman. *Behavior in Public Places: Notes on the Social Organization of Gatherings*[M]. New York: The Free Press，1966.

[8] Friederike Braun. *Terms of Address: Problems of Patterns and Usage in Various Languages and Cultures*[M]. Berlin: Walter de Gruyter，1988.

[9] J. M. Steadman, Jr. A Study of Verbal Taboo[J]. *American Speech*，1935: 10(2).

[10] Marvin Harris. *Good to Eat: Riddles of Food and Culture*[M]. Illinois: Waveland Press, Inc.，1998.

[11] Michael Argyle, Mark Cook. *Gaze and Mutual Gaze*[M]. Cambridge: Cambridge University Press. 1976

[12] Nicholas Antongiavanni. *The Suit: A Machiavellian Approach to Men's Style*[M]. New York: Harper Business，2006.

[13] Sue Fox. *Business Etiquette For Dummies*[M]. Indiana: Wiley Publishing, Inc，2008.

[14] Suzanne Von Drachenfels. *The Art of the Table: A Complete Guide to Table Setting, Table Manners, and Tableware*[M]. New York: Simon & Schuster，2000.

[15] 曹敏杰，马静波. 交际口语在线[M]. 大连：大连理工大学出版社，2003.

[16] 方汉文. 西方文化概论[M]. 北京：中国人民大学出版社，2006.

[17] (美)房龙著，刘乃亚，纪飞编译. *The Story of the Bible* 圣经的故事[M]. 北京：清华大学出版社，2008.

[18] (奥)格特鲁德·福森奈格编著.圣经故事[M]. 焦庸鉴，译. 北京：中国青年出版社，2009.

[19] 康志杰. 基督教的礼仪[M]. 北京：宗教文化出版社，2011.

[20] (美)玛格丽特·维萨著. 餐桌礼仪：文明举止的起源、发展与含义[M]. 刘晓媛，译. 北京：新星出版社，2007.

[21] 马云霞. 衣食住行英语会话[M]. 广州：世界图书出版公司，2009.

[22] 杨文慧. 商务礼仪英语[M]. 广州：中山大学出版社，2003.

[23] 虞苏美，李慧琴. 全新版大学英语听说教程[M]. 上海：上海外语教育出版社，2003.

[24] 赵擎天. 即学即用礼仪英语[M]. 北京：中国纺织出版社，2002.

图书在版编目（CIP）数据

西方社会礼仪与文化 / 范冰著．－杭州：浙江大学出版社，2014.11（2025.2 重印）
ISBN 978-7-308-13741-6

Ⅰ．①西… Ⅱ．①范… Ⅲ．①礼仪－西方国家
Ⅳ．① K891.26

中国版本图书馆CIP数据核字(2014)第198666号

西方社会礼仪与文化

范　冰著

责任编辑	陈丽勋	
责任校对	赵　坤	
封面设计	项梦怡	
出版发行	浙江大学出版社	
	（杭州市天目山路 148 号　邮政编码 310007）	
	（网址：http://www.zjupress.com）	
排　　版	杭州林智广告有限公司	
印　　刷	杭州高腾印务有限公司	
开　　本	787mm×1092mm　1/16	
印　　张	12.75	
字　　数	360 千	
版 印 次	2014 年 11 月第 1 版　2025 年 2 月第 8 次印刷	
书　　号	ISBN 978-7-308-13741-6	
定　　价	35.00 元	